What the Poem Wants
Prose on Poetry

Books by Michael Dennis Browne

The Wife of Winter
Sun Exercises
The Sun Fetcher
Smoke from the Fires
You Won't Remember This
Selected Poems 1964-1995
Give Her the River
Things I Can't Tell You
What the Poem Wants

What the Poem Wants
Prose on Poetry

by

Michael Dennis Browne

Carnegie Mellon University Press
Pittsburgh 2009

Acknowledgments

I am grateful to the editors of the following publications where these pieces, or versions of them, first appeared:

A View from the Loft; ARTS: The Arts in Religious and Theological Studies; Aspen Anthology; The Ohio Review; The Gettysburg Review; The True Subject: Writers on Life and Craft (Graywolf Press); *A Community of Writers: Paul Engle and the Iowa Writers' Workshop* (University of Iowa Press); *Religion and Contemporary Culture Series* (College of Saint Benedict).

I am grateful to the Graduate School and the College of Liberal Arts at the University of Minnesota for their support over the years.

Thanks to Nell Kromhout for her tireless, expert, and spirited work on these pages.

Thanks to the MacDowell Colony and the Collegeville Institute for their hospitality.

Thanks to my editor Gerald Costanzo for his support over thirty years.

Many of these pieces began as talks, and they span a period of thirty-five years. I have allowed myself some reuse of favorite quotations, aphorisms and anecdotes.

Book design by Graeme Ross-Munro

Contents

for my students

Henry Fermenting:
Debts to the Dream Songs

This started out as a "lone letter from a young man" ("Dream Song 342"). I intended to say something about my own sense of the achievement of the *Dream Songs*, something I was never able to do directly to John Berryman the few times I met him. In fact, one of the last times I saw him, I remember feeling very shy during our brief conversation, and wondering, later, whether I might ever feel enough at ease to tell him how much his work meant to me.

I don't know whether John Berryman would have been pleased to know of the extent to which his work affected my own at an important time in my writing life, but I like to imagine that he would. In the spring of 1971, at a poetry festival at Goddard College in Vermont, I introduced him to James Tate, whose first book, *The Lost Pilot*, had won the Yale Younger Poets' Prize for 1966, when Tate, at twenty-two, was the youngest poet ever to win the prize. And he told John Berryman that the epigraph for his book was the following:

> "Where did it all go wrong? There ought to be a law
> against Henry.
> —Mr. Bones: there is."

Berryman didn't know Tate's work, but he seemed delighted at this tribute from a younger poet.

So when I began working on this talk, it soon occurred to me that rather than recount merely my own debt to the achievement of those amazing poems, I should include that of other poets whose work I knew, or suspected, owed something to the *Dream Songs*. And so that this "lone letter from a young man" should form a wider tribute to a much-loved poet, I shall be quoting from eight or so other poets who replied to a letter from me with *their* own feelings about the poems.

My own experience of the *Dream Songs* has been something of a continuing journey toward them. When I first came to read them, in a seminar given by Donald Justice at the Iowa Writers' Workshop in the Spring of 1966, a group that included poets such as James Tate and Jon Anderson, I was young and English, and I had some very different kinds of diction in my head. I didn't know much of what was going on in the poems at all: they were tricky, and quite a few of them still are for me. I can't come near them. But I also take note of "Dream Song 366," where the poet says that the poems were not meant to be "understood"—"They are only meant to terrify & comfort."

And something in me at that time resisted them: the idiom was too eccentric to take root in the deepest places in my head, where the best poems have seemed to go. It wasn't until I heard John Berryman himself read from the *Dream Songs* in Iowa City in the Spring of 1968—the first time I had seen or heard him—that I began to feel the real power and energy of the poems.

He read them from the center of a large stage, to a large audience. He read them *slowly*—more slowly at times than I would have thought possible—but there were also variations within this slowness, sudden bursts and accelerations, sudden drastic increases in volume. And the poems came over to the audience with an extraordinary combination of authority and intimacy—a kind of lyrical power that I had not heard in spoken poetry before.

It's a common thing to say that certain poets *need* to be read aloud—in fact, insist on it (Hopkins, for example, or Roethke)—so that we feel the power of what Wordsworth once called, with the old inclusiveness, "a man speaking to men." And in our age, the oral act of poetry seems to us increasingly important—not a substitution for the encounter with the poem on the page, with all its spaces and silences, the way the eye is pulled through the varying lengths of the lines and over and into the places where the line is broken on the page—but as another way of encountering the poem, of hearing its voice in all its overtones, the direct human seriousness of its address to the reader. Berryman's poems came alive for me, dramatically so, when he said them aloud. And later, I could go back to them on the page and hear, always, that voice in my ear. What struck me then, at that reading, stays with me still—the extraordinary art of these poems, how such intimate material could be voiced with such authority of music, how so many curious, fearful details of someone's life and psyche—what he did, what he often subversively thought and conjectured—could be so memorably uttered.

What John Berryman does in the *Dream Songs* is not to pour out his secrets shapelessly, as some poets labeled, however crudely, "confessional," have done. Something in his nature and academic training, together with his obvious love for poetic form and the rigorous working of language, made him a poet to whom forms were natural allies, in somewhat the same measure as they were for his early master Auden, and certainly for Yeats, from whom, he claimed, he took the form of the three six-line stanzas of the *Dream Songs*. These were early masters for Berryman, because something in him clearly responded to that combination of passionate personal, often informal, utterance and formal memorable music which we hear in these poets.

My title, "Henry Fermenting," is maybe a curious one. As a friend said to me, it sounds like a proper name: "A Mr. Henry Fermenting to see you, sir." I was thinking of Stephen Spender's phrase about Gerard Manley Hopkins—"he ferments in other poets"—and this talk seemed to be an opportunity to find out the nature of that fermentation, for me and others, in the case of John Berryman. I felt it, but could not articulate it, just as, frequently, one writes a poem to *find out*, beginning, as Frost says, with merely "a lump in the throat." Or, as Auden says, quoting E. M. Forster, "How do I know what I think till I see what I say?"

Such an influence of a poet must surely be *indirect*. A direct influence would likely be a disaster. The good poet is inimitable. What one can learn is an atmosphere of mind, something communicating before understood, in Eliot's phrase, as from a poetry reading, for example, where you may retain just a few particulars but leave with a strong sense of energy and intimations of a stance toward experience (and the love of its means of expression in language) which can give one great joy and courage to go on. But as for direct influence, here is how Philip Levine put it:

> The *Dream Songs* are going to spawn a lot of cycles, and I suspect most of them will be too close to John, & bad. John was so singular a person & so much himself in those poems, that what his imitators come away with are all mannerisms. . . . And so I've loved those poems & left them alone. All that range in voices, in tones, diction—I've tried at times to get that in my poems. I really think John would say—"Levine, you crude bastard, leave me poems alone," for he laughed good naturedly when he caught me imitating others, & said how that was useful early on but how later you had to swim up your own blood-stream into the throat of your own demons.

And Michael Berryhill:

> It is obvious that one doesn't dare imitate Berryman the way, say, Berryman imitated Auden. Auden's voice was somehow respectably inimitable; imitation of Berryman lapses into parody.

And Keith Gunderson:

> I think I also felt immediately, however, that the poems were so singular in syntax, voice, and subject matter, that no young poet could try to borrow Berryman techniques successfully. Unlike, for example, W. C. Williams, or Pound, Berryman does not provide for other poets a fund of tactics or word tricks. One could not, I think, incorporate any of his major compositional strategies into his or her own writing without producing a bad and baldly obvious imitation of Berryman. (Dylan Thomas is comparably useless as a poet to filch from or imitate.)

I basically agree with these poets, but I would emphasize the point Berryman made to Levine, that there is a time in your writing life when imitation is desirable and, I would add, unavoidable. (I like what Maurice Ravel says: "Any composer who shows no influences should change his profession.") Any young poet's head is a mess of echoes; many voices are there, and s/he is kept busy sorting out sounds until the time when something singular begins to be heard. That time of subservience can lay strong foundations, but it can be a dangerous time, in which good writers may go under and not be heard from again. "More poets fail from lack of character than lack of intelligence," said Pound. And perhaps it is strength of personality, however indefinable, rather than intellect, which permits a young poet to resist, yet assimilate, and finally survive and bring out a distinctive voice. Certainly, John Berryman heaved Auden off his back—and Yeats, too, in a way which Theodore Roethke, at least later in his writing, did not (or chose not to).

So what can poets take, learn from the *Dream Songs*? How do we carry them on—and on our own terms? I'd suggest, first, that it's in the person of Henry that a large part of the answer lies. Who is Henry? Or, perhaps, what is Henry? He is, variously, huffy, reluctant, somber, stricken, disordered, miserable, willful, stunned, imperishable, anarchic, lonely, longing, completely exhausted, instant, horrible, foaming, seedy. He is also Henry Pussy-Cat, Henry Hankovitch, Henry of Donnybrook, Sir Henry, Henry House. He is Mr. Bones, Sir Bones. Sometimes, in my own head, I call him Calibones, or Sir Trombones, because he slides around so much. He is, in fact, the most comprehensive of souls, the very prince of picaresques, someone to whom everything happens, a man who wears his wounds openly, a man too vulnerable, who loves not wisely but too well. He has suffered an "irreversible loss," which we now know to have been the death of his father, by suicide, when he (Berryman/Henry) was still very young. He has been flung out of the garden, and in place of the tree of the knowledge of good and evil, which he has lost, he has made his own "flashing & bursting tree." He is one of the weirdest, most real, most endearing and most

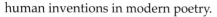

human inventions in modern poetry.

And, of course, he is a persona. He is not the poet; although, as Berryman once admitted, "There is a fiendish resemblance between Henry & me." Other poets have invented personae; as Donald Justice wrote to me:

> Like others of his period he was interested in
> inventing and projecting a dramatic voice or voices,
> the lyric mode for a time having been pulled by
> criticism toward the dramatic. Berryman did succeed
> in managing this better, I think, than anyone else
> does.

And for myself, I can think of no other whose invention is both so startling and so sustained. One thinks, of course, of Prufrock—"I grow old, I grow old, / I shall wear the bottoms of my trousers rolled."—and wonders what would have happened if he, Prufrock, rather than Eliot, had gone on to write the *Four Quartets*. But the fact is that Henry is quite our juiciest (anti-)hero and persona.

Now the inventing of a persona, the putting on of a mask, is a dangerous thing for a poet. Its rewards, as in the case of Henry, are huge; but it opens him to huge dangers. And Henry is, above all, open. The first line of the whole sequence—"Huffy Henry hid"—is, in this connection, completely ironic. But then comes the "prying open for all the world to see." The creating of a persona is, for the conscious mind, both unwelcome, in some sense, and a necessary extension of it. In the case of Henry, all kinds of material previously inaccessible was released and swarmed into the poems, much of it fearful, all of it vital. So much that previously was inexpressible could now find a voice, as the whole range of invention and language widened. The width, the range, are what immediately strike one in these poems.

And with a persona, one can begin to explore the furthest reaches of one's self, as Henry does here, fiercely, single-mindedly, but without narcissism, because the uncovering of this "other" is an essential psychic task which all of us must, to some extent, undertake, whatever the dangers. And Henry does it for us, and that is surely part of the immense reward of these poems, the sense of both identification and release, that someone does it, and does it for us. He falls apart for us; he does his dance in front of us. No one in American poetry since Roethke (with whose *Lost Son* poems, with their gibbering language and theme of flight from the death of the father, Henry has much in common) has so let down his brain, so pried himself open.

It is, paradoxically, the basic informality of the device which seems to make possible the access to much deeper material; the vast range of tone, from high to low, seems a sort of lubrication around the subject-matter and lays the poem open to bewildering shifts and changes of direction, so that we feel we are never prepared for what might come next. The poem is left open not only to the personal circumstances of the poet's life, as Berryman said, but also to the weather of the head, with all its sudden clearings and cloudings, all its visions and frustrations. The device of dialogue brings even more space into the poems and intensifies the sense of antithesis that runs throughout them. Every Prospero has his Caliban, every Eliot his Sweeney, every self his shadow. And Berryman has his Henry and his Henry another name, and there is yet another voice who addresses Henry, whose name we do not know.

It is the *life* these poems have, in the person of Henry, that is perhaps the most distinctive thing about them. Often I have come away from poems feeling, "*Surely* these poems are not the measure of the experiences; surely the fires were hotter, the waters wetter; surely there was more that could have been encountered, more brought back." But Henry's poems, with their extraordinary range of response to experience, with tears and laughter often summoned in swift succession, do frequently seem to be adequate equivalents for the intensity of the emotions involved in the original experi-ence. And the process of the poem, its speed and changes of speed, its mixtures of diction, make us feel that, yes, this is how the head works; and it is this fidelity to the process which we should note and learn from. Their language seems to be what William Meredith said of the Roethke poems, "the strange irrational language with which we talk to ourselves." And so we can identify, and so our own hidden pettinesses and shames are drawn up, as into a huge updraft, into the life of the poem.

One learns, as poet, as person, not to approach any situation or experience *too narrowly*. The stock response, whether tragic or lyrical, is never adequate to the actual dimensions, often submerged, of the experience. It is the use of the persona, him/herself previously submerged, that helps bring these dimensions to light and immeasurably widens and intensifies the poem.

A lot of ground is covered in Berryman's sequence. In "Dream Song 51," for example, he begins with cadences which are certainly Shakespearean ("Our wounds to time from all the other times"); the poem then shifts to the talk in blackface which runs in and out of the songs; then again a flash of Shakespeare; and then, who knows, Samuel Beckett, maybe ("Has you the night sweats and the day sweats, pal?"). I'm not at all calling the poem derivative, but merely suggesting the range of its tone.

In "Dream Song 382," there are similar shifts of diction and tone, with a discharging early on of the grander manner, and in the outrageous "Dream Song 44," originally written on a cocktail napkin in a Minneapolis restaurant, grander, even wickedly difficult, risks are taken. (The last line-and-a-half of this poem were Tate's epigraph for *The Lost Pilot*.)

The humorous, or semi-humorous, or ironic response to experience, done with this kind of vitality, is a complex one, and hard to achieve. It is a miracle that Berryman achieves it so often. And it is around this point that the remarks of many of the poets to whom I wrote seem to collect. Thom Gunn, an English poet at Berkeley, said:

> What I like about the *Dream Songs*, especially the first batch of them, is that they are *funny*. Berryman is beautifully aware of the comic aspects to Christianity, Catholicism, suicide, Freudianism, alcoholism, and the other planks that make up the strange homemade

box he is trapped in. His sense of humor is very
similar to Kafka's "The Burrow," even though he and
Kafka are opposites in style.

John McNally, a colleague at the University of Minnesota,
wrote:

The anguish in the poems is powerful and real, but
it is the delight in the midst of anguish that is most
real to me, and that comes, with Henry's help, to my
fingers. Hamm in Beckett's *Endgame* repeats "Ah
yesterday" with his parents dying in the ashcans.
Berryman says "hot diggety" to Emily Dickinson.
What else can a decent man do for that lady?

And William Meredith:

Berryman helped a lot of us to find the language we
needed to talk in poetry about what is new in our
culture.

It had happened again (it is always happening),
what Wordsworth complained about in the diction
of poetry at the end of the 18th century: "A language
was thus insensibly produced, differing materially
from the real language of men *in any situation*."
Berryman was one of the great revolutionaries in
this matter in recent American poetry, forty years
after Frost. We all needed to learn how to meld the
articulate low language of our time, the language that
handles directly the anger and humor and violence of
its time, with the traditional language of poetry. John
helped. His own style, moreover, was so inimitable
that one could only learn the hard way, letting him
nudge one towards one's own honest vulgar tongue.

That phrase, "one's own honest vulgar tongue," returns me
to the point I made earlier concerning the Roethke poems, that
one feels encouraged by the surfacing of such irrational and at

times ludicrous or infantile language to dig for the real words one needs to render joys and pains distinctively, and not settle for the old dictions.

It is, in fact, the play *against* these dictions which is the strength and variety of many of the poems. Donald Justice began by saying that "Berryman's work begins with an informed love of tradition accompanied by a nervous compulsion to test that tradition with experiment," and it is clear how important the meeting and even clashing of these two tendencies is. There is a constant erecting and canceling of lyricism, iambic formality and nervous metrical informality, a setting of fragment against flow. Robert Pinsky has written well on this topic in *The Situation of Poetry*. And it reminds me of a definition of melody I read once in a life of Beethoven by David Pryce-Jones: "a combination of cadence and surprise."

It's clear also that this sense of surprise was going on in John Berryman before the *Dream Songs*—perhaps particularly in "Homage to Mistress Bradstreet" and *The Nervous Songs*. Philip Levine wrote:

> A lot of things that happen beautifully in the *Dream Songs* John could articulate before he even wrote those poems. A certain way real & jagged speech plays off traditional rhythms. He made me hear that before he ever did himself, brilliantly. Made me love the art of hiding the art before he had that much art to hide.

And so here is the paradox stated again, the nature of dream material, released through the persona—maybe a cold term for Henry, but I can't think of another—together with the shape and form of song, the craft and art sorting the amazing material into an organic kind of order. To quote Donald Justice again:

> His subject was the self, often enough the self involved with history. But his personal exposures have a different feel about them than those of his contemporaries. No matter how painful and honest they seem, they have first been subjected to the

pressures of his art. Events, however catastrophic, are valued not so much for themselves as for what they can be made into, in words and music. The impersonality of the art remains, therefore, as important as the personality of the poet.

Justice speaks of the pressures of the art. These involve, among other things, the use of the three six-line stanzas, which, as Berryman said, was somewhat like writing an extended three-part sonnet; it gave him more room than in a sonnet, and the poems seem less intimidated by traditional expectations of structure and strategy. The syntax, too, comes under immense pressure, and is sometimes quite wrenched around under the intensity of what has to be said. For myself, I never felt the distortions of syntax to be any kind of eccentric imposition from outside, but rather a compulsive, essentially internal necessity, very much rising from the expressive needs of the poem. As Yeats says, "a passionate syntax for passionate subject matter."

On this point, and somewhat another, Marvin Bell wrote:

I am indebted to Berryman for extending the boundaries of the poetic self, for broadening the meaning of "diction," for risking syntax to achieve accuracy and logic forbidden the more conventional. His speaker in the *Dream Songs* defied and lusted and remembered and thought *hard*. Grace and restraint mixed with absolute *wanting* in a new way. And his work confirms the single location of the comic and the tragic.

It is, again and again, the sense of release these poets feel, that such material should be available and available poetically, available intuitively as poetry, as music. A poet can have few higher tasks than to extend the poetic idiom, to make the language we must all share increasingly expressive of our situations. Daniel Hughes wrote of Berryman's

intricate craft and impeccable ear. He turned around
the sloppy autobiographical poem of the late fifties
and early sixties without dragging us back to the
mausoleum of worn-out artifacts the poet needs to
hide from himself. As you intimate in your note, the
use and creation of Henry was the key. The message
went out and still throbs: Poets, Make Your Own
Henries—if you have the skill and guts to do so. Who
knows what your real name may be?

I have spoken of Henry, and the range of his experience.
Now I want to look at something only touched upon earlier—the
sheer music of many of the poems, that quality without which
a poem, however vital, can often be just a heap of information.
M. L. Rosenthal wrote of Yeats that "he had the simple indis-
pensable gift of enchanting the ear," and I would now take that
phrase and apply it to Berryman in the *Dream Songs*. It is a dif-
ficult art, this intuitive arriving of thought *as* music; few poets
can do it, very few in the modern age as John Berryman has
done. I've suggested that it is something often worked against
in the poems, but sometimes it flows for its own sake: a difficult,
direct kind of music, with little or no metaphor—pure speech,
pure recollection, its absence of metaphor an intention rather
than a lack, a poem trusting its own music.

In "Opus Posthumous No. 13," for example, Henry is quite
without the consolations of his customary vitality and is simply,
humanly sad, for himself, for us and all our losses: "but he could
try; / let it all rest, have a good cry." Such simplicity, close to
doggerel, is, in the context of the poem's frequently richer speech,
deeply affecting.

Michael Berryhill remarked:

In the example of his work is such a care for the word
itself, a care that I can only see as the love a painter
must feel when he has a tube of paint in his hand,
or the infinite love and guile with which Gaudier-
Breska approached a hunk of stone. He conveys that

obsession in his work, and I have carried that away from it.

One more point—an important one: Berryman was very emphatic in placing at the center of the *Dream Songs* the theme of the "irreversible loss," the death of the father. Daniel Hughes, writing to me on the subject of the elegiac element in the Dream Songs, called it

> Berryman's modern "Lament for the Makers." The pattern I traced in his work of Crisis, Lament and Prayer is most evident here. This elegiac center in Berryman is at once traditional and restorative; the deaths of poets and poet-friends are no more unfortunate than any other deaths, but for a poet reading them, Berryman's obsequies become ennobling moments of a kind of celebration—*one feels encouraged to go on* and I would want to put it that directly.

I'll quarrel a little with Hughes's statement that "the death of poets and poet-friends are no more unfortunate than any other deaths." It seems to me that the death of the father is such an under-cutting, such an undermining for the young sensibility, that the death of, indeed, poets and poet-friends, re-awakens to a large extent the same traumatic vibration, jangles the spirit equally, again and again, even into advancing age. As Dylan Thomas says, in a different context, "After the first death, there is no other."

In this connection, I think again of Roethke's *The Lost Son*, with its frantic attempts to exorcise such a death, the flight from the failure of the father to survive. I think—of course—of Joyce, and the search for the father. I think of James Tate's intuitively using an epigraph from the *Dream Songs* for a book whose title refers to his own vanished father before any one ever knew that the irreversible loss which sent Henry reeling through the world was the death of *his* father.

In my own poetic life, the poems I have written which owe

the most to the *Dream Songs* are a group called the Morley poems: the title is not a consciously chosen echo of Henry, but a name given to me by someone who had never heard of Henry. I wrote a large number of persona poems, which involved the kind of release and extension of self which I have spoken of earlier; it was only when I was six months into the poems, and close to finishing the sequence, that I came to realize consciously—as distinct from unconsciously—the significance of the name for me, that the place where my own father had died when I was nineteen years old was the Atkinson *Morley* hospital, that I was indeed Michael Morley, son of the place of the death of the father. "After the first death, there is no other."

The point I am hoping to make is that this confrontation with, this fleeing from, the death of the father, a vast theme in our literature, is one which Berryman approaches in these poems in a characteristically individual way. It is the source of his rage and desperation, the invisible worm that flies in the night; it is this he must have out with even more fiercely than with the ghosts of Yeats or Horace. His obsession with the theme reinforces, for the poet, its absolute centrality, the necessity for its confrontation and exorcism, like the core of the revolving earth itself which must be penetrated. Marvin Bell said:

> In the end, the *Dream Songs* surround a notion central
> to my own poems so far: the inescapable importance
> of the parent and the inevitable tragedy of the
> parent's fallibility.

In everything I have spoken of, I believe there is a sense of dimension—the space between the poet and the persona, the space between the beauty of the traditional diction and the joy in the nervous music of the new, the space between the delight in the new-born and the desire to assume the posture of the dead, in the bed, in the coffin. "Without contraries," Blake says, "is no progression." Such space permits Henry to say, "Working & children & pals are the point of the thing," and, in the next breath, with an utter sense

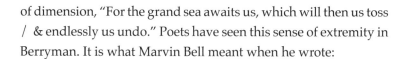

of dimension, "For the grand sea awaits us, which will then us toss / & endlessly us undo." Poets have seen this sense of extremity in Berryman. It is what Marvin Bell meant when he wrote:

> Finally, let me say that Berryman could be overcome in his poems. I felt, in writing myself a book-length sequence of short poems under great pressure, that the Henry of the *Dream Songs* had spotted for many of us a place nearer the edge where we might sit in near-safety.

And Philip Levine:

> From Bradstreet on he gave us great poetry & he wrote it right there where most of us can't stand to be, in hell. I think he's the greatest inspiration of his age & at his best he is the best.

And Donald Justice:

> So much of what he learned, practiced for, suffered and enjoyed was brought together in the *Dream Songs*, especially in the first book—his best—that I cannot help admiring him more than any other poet of his generation.

And so what then is the fermentation of Henry with which I began? I remember thinking, after I had first heard Berryman in person, that here was a poet who had discovered a marvelous way of talking about himself. I remember thinking that a poet must prepare her/himself, must be ready for the occasion when it comes, must love the language, must push it to all its possible effects while waiting for the occasion which summons it to its best use: in the words of Coleridge, "a more than usual state of excitement together with a more than usual state of order." When the occasion comes, as I believe it did for John Berryman in the *Dream Songs*, in the person of Henry, he must then trust that opening sense of himself; trust, also, that music of which he knows himself capable;

then he must follow the flow of invention, that single location of the tragic and comic, that jerked-open sense of the possibilities of experience and the linguistic utterance of it, the pain and fear, the joy and love, inextricable at source.

This is an edited version of a talk given at the opening of an exhibit of Berryman papers at the University of Minnesota Library, October 1973.

Coda: John Berryman

He was the greatest reader out loud of poetry I have heard. Also about the strangest. I thought I would tell you that only after saying "Dream Song 67" to you—just, I suppose, to do myself some small kind of protective favor.

We're here to celebrate him. To celebrate his way of moving the words around. When I read that dream song, I think of something Gauguin is supposed to have said after seeing a new painting by Van Gogh: "No one ever painted a chair like that before!" His freedom in and around a fixed form of his own choice, the way he pushes out the space from inside the sonnet tendency, are dazzling. I continue to feel freed and challenged by his example.

We're here to praise him, the unusually valuable Berryman. I've always loved what Bill Meredith wrote right after that difficult death: "As for me, I do what's in character; / I look for things to praise / along the river bank."

A lot of American poets have affected the English manner. As someone who left the English manner behind—or thought he did—and sought American poetry, I'm intrigued by the American hankering after English ways. The English don't own the pentameter, but certain Americans, as we know, have tried to smash it as if they did. John Berryman lusted greatly after that forbidden diction. He went over the water a number of times—to Cambridge, of course, to Ireland (on one occasion, as he immodestly said, to have it out with Yeats)—and writes memorably about the beginning of one such journey in "Dream Song 283," which ends " in love with life / which has produced this wreck," a lament almost Biblical in the anguish of its antithesis.

I was his colleague for a few months only, but I feel honored by the connection. Each teaching day, I walk by the building where he taught; I can see it from my west-facing window. As a bookmark in my copy of the *Dream Songs*, I keep a yellowed sheet of paper

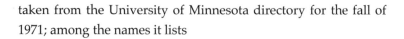

taken from the University of Minnesota directory for the fall of 1971; among the names it lists

> BERRYMAN, John,
> Regents' Professor,
> 354 Ford Hall, 373-3513.

When I cross the Washington Avenue Bridge, as I often do, I give thanks for his contribution to the art of poetry and wish his soul the bliss he sensed was possible, but never could live out here.

He was an exceptional teacher. Many have said it. Philip Levine, among others, has written absolutely brilliantly about that, and first spoke those words in his keynote address at the John Berryman conference we held in Minneapolis. And just two weeks ago, I picked up a copy of the latest issue of the University of Minnesota Alumni magazine, in which there is a feature on renowned teachers, and I read these words about him by Leonard Addington, class of '58, now an attorney in Minneapolis:

> He was the greatest teacher I ever knew. He showed
> a lot of respect, even admiration, for his students.
> He was very exciting, very intense, a lot of fun. He
> rarely spoke of his own work. Later, as I read some of
> his poetry, I saw the suffering and great unresolved
> grief of his life. He taught me to read the great
> poets as if they were writing for me personally. I
> will never forget him reading from Dante's Inferno,
> untranslated. His voice was shaking with emotion
> and tears rolled down his cheeks. It seemed that,
> before my eyes, one great poet was speaking to
> another. There was so much passion in his reading
> that it was startling.

I want to finish with his prose—the ending of his remarkable story "Wash Far Away," in which a professor has been struggling to teach Milton's great poem "Lycidas." I pick it up where the professor is reading from the poem:

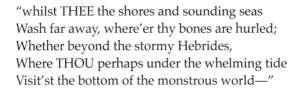

"whilst THEE the shores and sounding seas
Wash far away, where'er thy bones are hurled;
Whether beyond the stormy Hebrides,
Where THOU perhaps under the whelming tide
Visit'st the bottom of the monstrous world—"

The professor sat a long time in his office, not
thinking of anything and perhaps not unhappy, before
he went home. Once he read over the transfiguration
of Lycidas, and was troubled by the trembling of the
light on the page; his eyes had filled with tears. He
heard the portrait's voice. At last he rose, closed the
window, and took his hat. Shutting the door as he left,
in the still-bright hail he looked at the name engraved
on his card on the door. He felt older than he had
in the morning, but he was moved into the exacting
conviction that he was . . . something . . . not dead.

80th birthday celebration for John Berryman,
The New School, New York, November 1994.

Gods Beyond My God:
The Poetry of D.H. Lawrence

I first read the novels and many of the shorter works in high school in England; they introduced me a world I knew I would never leave—everything intensely vivid, so hugely conceived. In college, I began on the poems, and was entranced; I had never read anything more *alive* than the poems in *Birds, Beasts and Flowers* or more movingly solemn than "The Ship of Death" and other late poems. Ever since, he has been in me as a writer.

With "Fish," written at Zell-am-Zee, a lakeside town in Austria, in its journey from the opening "Fish, oh Fish, / So little matters!" through "You and the naked element, / Sway-wave. / Curvetting bits of tin in the evening light." to "They are beyond me, are fishes" and on to the poem's conclusion, in which Jesus is invoked, I knew I was in the presence of a master describer, a master mariner, who could go almost wherever he wanted in poems, and in a range of tones that drew all manner of colors out of the English language while keeping its base unmistakably in the colloquial. I loved the surge of the poem, Lawrence's animal-like ability to stop, start again, stop, start again, all of it seemingly effortlessly managed. Such freshness; such progressive astonishment; such discovery.

So since that first encounter, at eighteen, in a raw northern city (Hull), I have loved Lawrence's poetry, and that poem in particular. In the best work, I always feel in the presence of the poet's own surprise. And it is in the poems of non-human life in *Birds, Beasts and Flowers*, such as "Fish," that Lawrence came for the first time truly into his own as a poet. They are like no other poems he had done before, and unlike anything else in our tradition—not like Blake or Clare or Wordsworth, none of those (whom I loved also). With these writings, he was not only breaking from the poetic conventions and forms he grew up in, but was entering new terri-

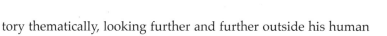

tory thematically, looking further and further outside his human self for fragments of the mystery: "gods beyond my god."

In the search for wholeness, we have to do a great deal of unlearning as we come toward a new way of seeing our universe. Lawrence always knew this, he was possessed by the notion, but in his earlier work in poetry he could not enact it, he lacked the tools. But in the creature and fruit and flower and tree poems, he was looking with increasing energy at what was not him-self, *Nicht-Ich*, those presences that live so powerfully, in silence, beyond the limits of human ego-personality. He was hungry and thirsty for the mystery, and it was these phenomena he was now beginning to consult more and more: oracles of the non-human. Lawrence always felt himself a part of something larger, and passionately wished for connection with it. In his preface to the *Collected Letters*, Aldous Huxley writes of Lawrence that "He had eyes that could see, beyond the walls of light, far into the darkness, sensitive fingers that kept him continually aware of the environing mystery . . . he did not want to increase the illuminated area; he approved of the outer darkness, he felt at home in it."

For Lawrence, darkness was a favorite word, a symbol of many connotations, but in large measure it represented the Unknown. "I am mad for the unknown," he once said. But he also knew that he could not reach out and grab that darkness and pull it to him. Nor could he summon its representatives; all he could do was to invite them to approach and enter him. In an essay on Benjamin Franklin in his *Studies in Classic American Literature*, he writes of the soul as a forest, with the self no more than a clearing in it, and that "gods, strange gods, come forth from the forest into the clearing of my known self, and then go back. . . . I must have the courage to let them come and go."

That central notion is, for me, such a vivid evocation of the state of mind that can initiate the making of a poem. Although entirely different in terminology, it is not unlike Keats' formulation of negative capability, that state in which we are capable of being in "uncertainties, mysteries and doubts without any irritable reaching after fact and reason." It reminds me, too, of Wordsworth's "wise passiveness" or of Dylan Thomas' "I let an image be made in me." In a poem from *More Pansies*, a later volume, Lawrence writes of gods that exist or do not exist, "according to the soul's desire, / like a pool into which we plunge, or do not plunge."

There are many questions within the body of the poem "Fish." Lawrence was good at questions; it seems an intuitive dramatic device for him. And in the poems of *Birds, Beasts, and Flowers*, it is the physical, non-human, phenomenological world which is so large a source of the numinous for him—a question to live, in Rilke's sense, rather than to try to answer. Richard Ellmann calls this direction in Lawrence "an attempt to put human subjectivity in its place by showing the myriad of queer, separate, non-human existences around it," a slightly tart way of putting it, and certainly less luscious than Huxley, but the point is a good one, and emphasizes again Lawrence's intimation that the known self, the "old stable ego" as he called it, is an island in a sea vaster than we can imagine, that it covers only as much acreage as, say, the footprints of the recent first astronauts upon the surface of the moon.

Now this notion is not a new one; it is ancient, known in many traditions. But what I think distinguishes Lawrence in this regard is the intensity and evocativeness of his vocabulary, together with the inexhaustible quality of his searching as he sought, again and again, for expression of the unknown. Artists have always looked intently at the physical world; no object has ever been too humble as a source of revelation—Christ's inviting us to consider the lilies of the field, for example, or Yeats' "The rivers of Eden are in the midst of our rivers," or Blake's " A world in a grain of sand, / Heaven in a wild flower." With Lawrence, it is an obsession pursued with unusual energy in unusually consistent territory. The cypress, the fig tree, the almond, the anemone, the hibiscus, the mosquito, the fish, the bat, the snake, the tortoise, the lizard, the lion, the turkey-cock, the humming bird, the eagle, the ass, the dog, the he-goat, the she-goat, the elephant, the kangaroo, the red wolf—the list is generous, and generously comprehensive of creation. Jessie Cham-

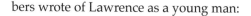
bers wrote of Lawrence as a young man:

> He was always to me a symbol of overflowing life.
> He seemed able to enter into other lives and not only
> human lives. With wild things, flowers and birds,
> a rabbit and a snare, the speckled eggs in a hole in
> the ground, he was in primal sympathy—a living
> vibration passed between him and them, so that I
> always saw him, in the strictest sense of the word,
> immortal.

One strong result of this "primal sympathy" between Lawrence and the creatures and objects of creation is that he does not mechanically use them and press them into symbolic service. Some poets evoke an object of nature only to interpret up, hopping from it promptly into the cosmic. In the "Fish" poem, on the other hand, we arrive finally at Jesus, by way of gods and other allusions, but it's clear that Lawrence saw the fish for itself, focused on seeing and riding out on his seeing, wherever it might take him.

When I was an undergraduate, I remember being told that symbols were things "that stood for things," and only subsequently, during various experiences—climbing the steps of Yeats' tower at Thoor Ballylee, for example, or hearing the wind through the pines by Lawrence's grave in the Lobo Canyon—did I come to feel the limits of such a well-intended definition. Often the symbol begins in obsessive image—the term is from Joseph Warren Beach—a physical presence whose recurring begins to send you out past itself for its implications, but remains a palpable identity which we must respond to in its physical essence.

Lawrence seemed often content to *see*, to see so vividly that we see with him. And so many times this happened in New Mexico, a landscape of which he said: "I think New Mexico was the greatest experience I have ever had . . . the moment I saw the brilliant, proud morning shine high over the deserts of Santa Fe, something stood still in my soul, and I started to attend." In his poem "Blue Jay," he moves from his dog—" Oh, Bibbles, little black bitch in the snow, /

With a pinch of snow in the groove of your silly snub nose" to the common bird itself, of whom he asks: *"What voice of the Lord is that, from the tree of smoke?"* The pine tree in the poem is the same one he mentions in his luminous essay *Pan in America*, the same one that Georgia O'Keeffe painted and that still stands outside the cabin in the Lobo Canyon; he describes it as, by night, an Egyptian column stretching up into darkness; and by day, he says, "it is just a tree." How easily, authentically, he moves between worlds.

Thinking of the pine reminds me of one of Lawrence's natural successors in American poetry, Robert Bly, a poet who also has an exceptional eye for the physical world (and an uncanny one for the inner). In the preface of a recent book of prose poems, *The Morning Glory*, which contains poems about seals and grass and rain and rocks and tumbleweed and a range of natural objects, Bly says: "If we examine a pine carefully, we see how independent it is of us. When we first sense that a pine tree really doesn't need us, that it has a physical life and a moral life and a spiritual life that is complete without us, we feel alienated and depressed. The second time we feel it, we feel joyful." And I think of Lawrence and the fish: "I left off hailing him. / I had made a mistake, I didn't know him."

I feel I have learned so much from Lawrence in this, to look at something, to attend to it, and to leave well alone—no possessiveness of the kind Lawrence objects to in Wordsworth, whom he attacks with a typical mixture of truth and preposterousness in regard to the primrose: "William gathered it into his own bosom and made it part of his own nature. 'I, William am also a yellow primrose blossoming on a bank.' . . . This is bunk. A primrose has its own peculiar primrosy identity, and all the oversouling in the world won't melt it into a Williamish oneness."

Let me redress the balance back just a little toward what is, in fact, symbolic, the inward implication of the physical (what David Bohm terms "the implicate order"). However exquisite a poet of nature John Clare, for example, may be—and I love his writing— one misses from it, finally, the pressure of the invisible. He has just about the clearest physical eye of any poet in English literature, but he did not often enough go, at least for me, beyond description. But Lawrence's world encompasses the duality of Jesus and the fish, of the snake and the gods. And the gods were what he wanted, the company he wished to keep, the representatives of the mystery, the "three strange angels," for example, of the poem "The Song of a Man Who has Come Through."

"Not I, but the wind." "Gods beyond my god." And the message of these angels is the same as it was for Rilke (by way of the torso of Apollo): "You must change your life." And why change? Because we have lost something; our lives have become contracted, covered over. In the more nervy and conscious poems in *Nettles* and *Pansies*, the theme of loss is often overt; in the creature poems, it is more implicit, as the intensity of attention implies its opposite. It is, to say it again, an ancient theme he is sounding. When Lawrence writes "We are all like tortoises who have to smash their shells and creep forth tender and over-vulnerable, but alive," I think back to Angelus Silesius, the seventeenth century German poet, who wrote, "My body is a shell, from which a chicken will be hatched from the spirit of eternity," and back more centuries to Meister Eckhart: "If you want to have the kernel, you must crack the shell." Lawrence is one more strong singer of this theme. He was raised in a society of trapped people—toilers and slaves, like his Plutonic father. Even much later, as he sat in the sun of the American southwest, he was back there in his mind in England with the mill hands and miners, breathing the bad air, doing their backbreaking work, thinking of them hauled into work every morning like fish with hooks in their mouths, as he wrote.

In these remarks, I'm not stressing the poems of social anger, or satire, or love, or the dialect poems: these are powerful components of Lawrence's poetic personality, but I'm staying true to the chief elements of my own delight in his work. When Lawrence condemns and preaches, he is often strident; when he celebrates, then he is magical. In *Etruscan Places*, he writes:

> [Man is striving for] one thing, life, more and more
> of the gleaming vitality of the cosmos . . . the active

religious idea was that man, by vivid attention and subtlety and exerting all his strength, could draw more life into himself, more and more glistening vitality, till he became shining like the morning, blazing like a god."

Carl Jung also writes on this theme, of how we have lost our contact with nature, "and with it has gone the profound emotional energy that this symbolic connection supplied."

But Lawrence persistently addresses, and even questions, stones, plants and animals. Of trees, he asks: "Tuscan cypresses, what is it?" And to the moon he says: "Come up, thou red thing. / Come up, and be called a moon." And to the turkey cock: "You ruffled dark blossom, / You glossy dark wind." He asks the mosquito: "When do you start your tricks, / Monsieur?" And to the tortoise he says: "You know what it is to be alone, / Baby Tortoise!" And of course: "Fish, oh Fish, / So little matters!"

In his prose, he wrote: "Thought is not a trick, or an exercise, or a set of dodges. Thought is man in his wholeness wholly attending." In the essay *Chaos in Poetry*, he wrote: "The essential quality of poetry is that it makes a new effort of attention and 'discovers' a new world within the known world." And I have learned from him, as a person, as a poet, to look more closely and openly at the world. Reading his vividness, I feel ashamed at the pallor of my own vision. As W. H. Auden said of him: "To a fig tree or a tortoise he gives that passionate personal attention usually offered by lonely or shy people, or by children, invalids, prisoners, and the like; the others are too busy, too accustomed to having their own way."

While originally preparing these remarks, last fall, I read an account in the Minneapolis paper about an Englishwoman, Sheila Hocken, who lived in Nottingham (where Lawrence went to school), had been blind from birth, and had never seen colors, and only the very vaguest of shapes. One day, she began to be able to see, and when her sight was completely restored, she said this:

It was like an electric shock, really. It is almost

indescribable. White first, the nurse's apron. It was so dazzlingly bright, I had to turn away. There were so many colors; green, dark and pale, and royal blue. I didn't imagine the world was such a beautiful place. Now I am always astounded that people are not always going on about how wonderful things are.

When I go out, I say "Isn't the grass green? Did you see the sunset last night?" People are not interested. I suppose they take it all for granted . . . . When I first came out of the hospital, the real world was as if it had never been there before, had all been invented just for me. And I saw this green stuff on the ground—I could not believe it was grass. I had to touch it. And I had not imagined that trees grew everywhere and were all different shapes. . . . Another fascinating thing is water. Even now, when I turn the tap on, it is fascinating. It gleams and glistens and swirls down the sink. It is so many different colors, especially if you are outside and the sun is on it.

When I get up in the morning, it is marvelous. It is another day, and what am I going to see today? It is so fantastic to go out and think, "A few more flowers might have come out today. This is the life, this is the world, this is living!"

To read Lawrence's "Trees in the Garden," for one example, is to encounter a similar intensity: "all strangers to one another / as the green grass glows upwards, strangers in the silent garden."

I want now to look briefly at Lawrence's poetic career, both before and after *Birds, Beasts, and Flowers*. A great deal of his early work was really awful stuff, and certainly Lawrence is one of our most uneven poets; it's easy to skim him and come away thinking he was one of the dullest, most hopelessly loose of writers. It takes the courage of the true admirer to read through much of that early work, in which he was, as he himself wrote later, "struggling to say things it takes a man twenty years to be able to say." The forms are frequently forced and do not fit the thought—he was very awkward in his Georgian clothes and only intermittently convincing as an Imagist. The dialect poems, which Ezra Pound liked better than any other poems Lawrence wrote, are of some, but not deep, interest to me. Lawrence describes this early work as, again, the work of a young man, who, afraid of his demon, puts his hands over the demon's mouth and speaks for him. And then, he said, "It was after that, when I was twenty, that my real demon would now and then get hold of me and shake some more real poems out of me, making me uneasy."

It is encouraging for the apprentice poet, such as myself, to see how poorly a great poet can write (and sometimes so frequently). It should give us all hope! It is always a poignant time in a young poet's career, to glimpse those patches of promise amid the debris of the rest. I am reminded of Rilke's remark, in the first of his *Letters to a Young Poet*, when he says of a certain sonnet written by the apprentice writer: "There something of your own wants to come through to word and melody." Lawrence himself was to come through, and magnificently. But not yet!

Though there are individually fine earlier poems, such as "Piano," in which he was unafraid to show direct sentiment—and others such as "Love on the Farm," "Snapdragon," and "Aware"— the mass of it is weak. Auden puts it rather politely: "One is continually struck by the originality of the sensibility and the conventionality of the poetic means," and an English critic, Keith Sagar, somewhat less so: "The heart sinks on every rhyme word. Just as a poem begins to spread its wings, the first rhyme will bring it to the ground with a dull thud." But Lawrence always knew that there was something other in him, that his demon would come through. Others sensed it, too, but didn't know quite how to treat him. He said of them: "They were always telling me that I had got genius, as if to console me for not having their own incomparable advantages." If he did not yet have his own forms, still he knew that he must, and would, go beyond the orthodoxy of his time. In a letter to Edward Marsh—who went under the rather charming nickname "the Policeman of Poetry"—he wrote: "Remember—skilled verse is dead in fifty years."

It was after Lawrence had gone off to Europe with Frieda, the wife of a former teacher of his, that he began the poems which form the volume *Look! We Have Come Through!*, poems written between about 1914 and 1917. And here we begin to see more of the directness and freshness and range that characterize his later work in poetry. These poems excited, if that is the right word, a good amount of critical attention, much of it hostile. There was a good deal of sensuality, which was not at all to the British taste of the time. ("The English," Malcolm Muggeridge once said, "have sex on the brain, which is a very bad place to have it.") And Lawrence paid the price for this, as he did later when his paintings were declared obscene and the exhibition was closed down. The anonymous critic of *The Times Literary Supplement* wrote of the book: "[It is] an excited morbid babble about one's own emotions which the Muse of poetry can surely only turn from with pained distaste." Auden, who generally admires Lawrence very much, wrote that these poems made him feel as if he had opened the wrong door, like a Peeping Tom; Ezra Pound called the work "a sort of pre-raphaelitish slush, disgusting or very nearly so," and Bertrand Russell was heard to say, "They may have come through but I don't see why I should look."

But there are other views of this book (of which I am myself intermittently fond). Horace Gregory wrote about Lawrence's journey to this point in his life: "and at last the new man waking by his wife's side, her breasts the new world's mountains and the hollows of her body its valleys, and its orifices the deep mystery of oblivion and resurrection." The physical feeling was coming more and more into the poems, that sense of inscaped landscape so particular to Lawrence, of which Kenneth Rexroth wrote many years later: "I have never stood beside a glacier river . . . without hearing again the specific hiss of Lawrence's Isar." (The Isar was one of the rivers by which he walked with Frieda.) And this is the kind of legacy any poet could wish for, to be present in the body and mind of those who come after, to be actual for them and helpful to their own lives on the same path; not possible for poets to die when they are resurrected over and over again in the words and spirit of living writers. For Lawrence, one of whose chief symbols was the Phoenix, how much might such thoughts as Rexroth's have meant to him?

The First World War, of which Horace Gregory spoke, had badly hurt Lawrence's soul, and the hurt shows strongly in *Women in Love*, arguably his greatest novel, in which there are several interesting parallels between the passionate dialogues of Birkin and Ursula and some of the love poems in this volume. The war certainly led him to focus the intensity of his hope on the astonishing, revealing relationship with Frieda—and later also to turn to the world of birds, beasts and flowers, nonhuman presences which had played no part in the terrible human degradations of those four years. But in all the rush and ecstasy of new loving, Lawrence and Birkin both were seeking a balance, a "star-equilibrium," a respect of otherness in the human partner, a respect he showed later, as I've said, for his non-human "neighbors," as Auden calls them. Here, too, he watches, without swamping. In the extraordinarily tender poem "Gloire de Dijon," he lingers to watch Frieda washing, his attention at the least painterly—"And the sunbeams catch her / Glistening white on the shoulders." And while there are still traces of the older diction, the older ways he had still to shed, this is a poem more clearly of the new, fresh directness, as is "A Young Wife," which begins: "The pain of loving you / Is almost more than I can bear." So much is, for him, as he writes in the poem "Green," "now for the first time seen."

At other times, the tender and observant looking is replaced by a more gathered music, a visionary sense of relationship not only with the woman he loves but with all things: "We shall not look before and after. / We shall *be, now*. / We shall know in full. / We, the mystic NOW," he writes in the eighth and last section of "Manifesto."

There is a quality in Lawrence's writing, which one finds also in Robert Bly (whom I have called one of Lawrence's natural successors), a very distinctive kind of emotional and tonal directness. It is a quality which, together with the physical energy of the poems, has always excited me, and strongly influenced my own work (I do not claim virtue by association!). One of the most fatuous things someone can say to a poet is something like: "Oh, so you're a poet. OK then, talk poetry." But in a better sense, Lawrence really does talk poetry, or rather, he learned to. Gradually discarding the more traditional music, he built something else into his ways of saying. For me, there is a wonderfully vivid confiding and talking quality in his poetry, with little glaze of rhetoric. The English critic Alfred Alvarez once defined Lawrence's poems as "improvisations at the full pitch of his intelligence," and also said: "it was the utterance, what he had to say, which was poetic; not the analyzable form and technique. So for all his trouble, he never innovated in Pound's or Eliot's way." David Daiches says something similar, that Lawrence was not concerned with a poetic tradition but with a more general discovery of the truth.

We are here at the notion of Beyond Poetry, and it is dangerous ground. I think of Marianne Moore's poem "Poetry," which begins with the line "I, too, dislike it," or the words of Wilfred Owen, killed a week before the end of World War I, who wrote in the intended preface to his poems:

> Above all I am not concerned with Poetry.
> The poetry is in the pity.
> All a poet can do today is warn.

But surely poetry is craft? What if the person involved in such an enterprise is not a genius (as Lawrence surely was)? In a letter to Edward Marsh, Lawrence wrote: "I have always tried to get an emotion out in its own course, without altering it. It needs the finest instinct imaginable, much finer than the skill of the craftsman." And elsewhere he wrote:

> When observation is of the self, and of the self acting
> and suffering, it is never quite pure; never therefore, a
> real principle of control. But observation if it reaches a

sufficient intensity, can become a true discipline when it is of something objective, outside the self.

And this is not only dangerous but mysterious territory. Alvarez, who has called Lawrence "the foremost emotional realist of the century," comes back to the same subject:

> The whole of Lawrence's power and originality
> as a poet depends on the way he keeps close to
> his feelings. That is why he had to rid himself of
> conventional forms. The poems take even their shape
> from the feelings.

Now this is a quality I love in Lawrence, the way he talks and shapes at the same time. Tom Marshall, in a book on Lawrence's poetry, talks of:

> The idiom that is peculiarly his own; it is the almost
> matter-of-fact tone as much as the vision that
> gives even the briefest of these poetic thoughts its
> characteristic shape and unity.

It is almost amusing now—though, perhaps, still not quite—to see what a fuss all this caused in some critics of an earlier time. Eliot, for example, not at all attuned by personal temperament to Lawrence's strange gods, found that, technically, the poems were "very interesting amateur work; [it] is only notes for poems." And R. P. Blackmur, in the best-known attacking essay, calls Lawrence's poems "the ruins of great intentions, ruins we should however, admire and contemplate." Pretty warm ruins, I say.

Many have replied to this kind of charge, but I think the best thing to do is point to the poetic practice of the almost fifty years since Lawrence's death and to see there, as the mainstream mode of expression, just that kind of form—expressive, open, organic, whatever we now call it—which Lawrence preached and practiced so early and for which he received so much abuse. It is not mysterious to us now. It is not more dangerous than any other kind of artistic undertaking. The intuitive skills of the real artist, that unprecedented conjunction of eye and ear and blood and rhythm, are not so easily categorized and labeled as many critics would have us believe. It is not mysterious to us now, and, of course, it is completely mysterious; we do not have the terminology for it. I am content, more or less, with Robert Creeley's formulation, "Form is never more than an extension of content," which Denise Levertov later modified to "Form is never more than an *revelation* of content." This is how, now, in large part, it seems to be done. Intensities provide expressive shape; forms are a function of the poem's meaning.

What Lawrence had, of course, was a severe case of Whitmanitis. "Whitman has meant too much to me," wrote Lawrence, "Whitman, the one man breaking the way ahead." He called him "the pioneer, the white aborigine." And both Whitman and Lawrence are brothers, not least in the way they were attacked for their new notions of form.

I'm coming now to the *Last Poems*. To get there, one has to go by way of *Nettles* and *Pansies*, and with some exceptions, this is pretty flat stuff, much of it very bitchy, obvious, verbally undistinguished. ("The English Are So Nice," from *More Pansies*, is perhaps my favorite little slice of malevolence.)

Why Lawrence wrote often so badly is a subject for another time. Keith Sagar puts it chastely: "Lawrence wrote nearly 1000 poems, and we must concede that an unusually high proportion are unsuccessful." And yet some critics can retrieve value from the badness. Graham Hough writes: "One moment he is all thumbs, and the next he tells us something which we ignore at our peril." Vivian de Sola Pinto, one of the editors of the *Collected Poems*, claims "Like Wordsworth, he wrote a good deal of bad poetry, but, like Wordsworth's, even his bad poems are important because they are the experience of a major poet groping his way toward the discovery of a new kind of poetic art." And Alvarez writes that "It took genius and great courage even to fail in that way. When Lawrence's poems are bad they are victims of that peculiar honesty which, at other times, made for their strength."

And there it is again, the duality of Lawrence, the "impurity" as Neruda might call it. In that search for a new poetic art, "the poetry of the present" as he formulated it in the preface to the American edition of *New Poems*, he wanted the unevenness, the mixing of the fragmented and the whole, he wanted what he called the living plasm, nothing perfect or completed. And so it was not his ineptitude but his aesthetic which, in part, produced such an uneven body of work.

Alvarez speaks in his same essay on Lawrence of "the vanishing point of poetry." When it came to the vanishing point of Lawrence's own life, prematurely, in his early 40s (he was almost the same age as Chekhov; at the time of his death, he weighed eighty-five pounds), his courage and honesty and genius did not fail him. He clearly knew he was dying and the *adumbratio*, as Jung calls it, the anticipatory shadow, was casting its dark light over his psyche. Critics and poets who had despaired at the kind of utterance they found in *Nettles* and *Pansies* were amazed at how his genius now flowered. Richard Aldington wrote: "How good it is to know that the great and lovely spirit had always been there . . . that when he came to face the last reality, it was the beauty in him that found a new voice of grandeur and dignity. And Horace Gregory, after abhorring *Pansies*, wrote that it was "remarkable that the half-dozen magnificent poems of the last book should suddenly grow out of the refuse of the *Pansies*."

Lawrence was now facing something entirely new. And as he had learned and looked and studied along the way, as he had laid foundations of observing in the non-human poems on which I have laid such emphasis, so those acts of attention now bore fruit in his final poems, his most human poems, as he himself, feebler physically but as vividly seeking as ever inside, now became a central character in his own vision, and, as always, in the context of the gods and gods waiting in the darkness beyond his living life. "Ripeness is all." And perhaps only that can describe Lawrence at this point, ripe, close to falling, acquiescing, trying to prepare himself for a totally unknown experience, to give himself up, to make his own ritual of initiation for the most mysterious of passages. Even here, especially here, he must be open, he must let the wind blow through him, he must admit the angels at the door. In his greatest work, he harvested his earlier acts of attention, and that harvesting, I believe, is a lesson for all poets.

Part of the preparation was forgetting, a kind of shedding and turning to a new direction. Six months before he died, he wrote to his friend Lawrence Pollinger: "Very still and sunny here . . . Olvidar—vergessen—oublier—dimenticare—forget—so difficult to forget." This was in September 1929, the month in which he wrote "Bavarian Gentians." In this poem, as the poet tries to turn to face the new experience, the little Alpine flowers slip effortlessly into symbolism, becoming the instruments for guidance on the last journey. (These poems were found in Lawrence's notebooks, in his handwriting, and there are alternative versions of them.)

These last poems have haunted and accompanied my life since I first read them as a young student in England now almost twenty years ago, because they seem to me true, to have that great truth of feeling that one finds in Lawrence, no tricks or devices or dodges, and indeed no self-pity, but "a man in his wholeness wholly attending." They seem to me noble poems, poems of a curious and radical purity, a radical nobleness. To learn to concentrate all one's vision on what is happening, to bring one's gift to hear, to cause the seemingly single event to flare out into an aura of significances—that is another of the learning legacies and achievements of D.H. Lawrence. And it is amazing to me how, in this work, so sick a man could still so persist. It amazed Aldous Huxley, too, who said of Lawrence at this time: "For the last two years he was like a flame burning on in miraculous disregard of the fact that there was no more fuel to justify its existence . . . the flame blazing away, self-fed, in its broken and empty lamp."

As he grew weaker, the gods grew stronger about him and he felt their presences, the gods coming toward him over the Aegean from which they had sprung, Dionysus himself leaning on his gate, and there above him the moon, whom he prayed to make him whole. The old rituals came to his aid, the archetypes, the ancient patterns. "Have you built your ship of death, oh have you? / Oh build your ship of death, for you will need it," he asks at the beginning of one of the drafts of "The Ship of Death."

There are many things I have left unsaid or not been able to say; there are many more complexities and contradictions in Lawrence I have not tried to approach. But I hope I have given some sense of a poet I love more than most, who was onto something very serious, which answers to so much in my own searching. He was not an easy man, and I'm sure he couldn't stand a talk such as this, me with my semi-posh voice standing here trying to hand you all kinds of emotions! But I have learned so much from him and have tried to apply it in my writing, my teaching, my life. He wrote: "An act of pure attention, if you are capable of it, will bring its own answer." In the great poem "Shadows," the act of attention was upon his own dissolution, the spirit in the failing body capable of new wisdoms, of thinking itself into rebirth on the very edge of loss, "new blossoms of me," as he calls it, capable of confronting that loss of self he so aspired to and was, at the same time, humanly in awe of. The poem concludes:

> then I must know that still
> I am in the hands [of] the unknown God,
> he is breaking me down to his own oblivion
> to send me forth on a new morning, a new man.

A talk given in Minneapolis, November, 1976,
and subsequently at Colorado Mountain College
in Aspen, August, 1977.

My James Wright

James Wright was a rather pale young man and slender in build—in fact he was downright wispy, about as substantial as marsh gas—and he floated over the landscape, murmuring his frail poems to the breeze, before returning home for tea in his American Grantchester, somewhere in the Midwest, wherever that was, in time for, if not honey, maybe nectar or molasses.

This was my first impression of James Wright, my first misreading of him, in the spring of 1964. I was living in Finland, in Helsinki, and I had begun to read American poets in the U.S.I.S. library, among them Theodore Roethke, Robert Bly, Anne Sexton, William Stafford, Galway Kinnell, and James Dickey. Right away, I felt the call of American images and rhythms and moods, felt that "frisson nouveau," the new shiver Victor Hugo claimed he felt when he read Baudelaire for the first time. T. S. Eliot says that for all the love we have of the older literature, those traditions that nourish us, there is something about the literature of your own time that is peculiarly exciting. Reading those poets, new to me, who were writing from out of the New World, I loved Roethke especially, with his irresistible rhythms, his relishing of things, his ecstasy, Roethke who had died just the August before. But when I read James Wright for the first time—and it was either in *The Lion's Tail and Eyes* or in Donald Hall's *Contemporary American Poetry* anthology—I could not believe how beautiful the poems were. I read them again and again, and back in England, in the summer of 1964, I bought the Hall anthology and took it everywhere with me. I had never encountered anything like those poems. Reading them, I did not pick up on a lot of their darkness at first, but I did detect something lonely in them, and I was ready for some American loneliness.

The images and the syllables haunted me. I wanted the world they showed. There are those who set out to seek their fortune in the form of a crock of gold at the foot of a rainbow, but I wanted to locate those blazing horse droppings between two pines, some-where in the middle of the unknown America. For all my love of the English poetry I was raised on, starting with Chaucer, and of French poetry in college—the astonishing Baudelaire—and for all my slightly removed admiration of such contemporary English poets as Ted Hughes and Philip Larkin, nothing spoke to me quite so unmistakably as the poems of James Wright. They seemed to be what I had been dreaming to hear. That is how I want to write, I said to myself, and in a way, that is how I had been trying to write before I ever read those poems. In the fall of 1964, Paul Engle sent me a blue airmail letter with a large red maple leaf in it: "Next year you can see for yourself," he said. And so I did, with a seeing altered forever by James Wright's seeing. August 1965, the same summer that James Wright left Minnesota for good, I came to America.

I very much liked the Iowa landscape I found myself in—the rolling farm country, the huge sky—but it seemed rather different from the landscapes of James Wright's poems. Reading him in Fin-land, with its lakes and rocks and birches and pines, I had felt very close to the northern images, and now I wanted to see that territory for myself. Some friends had a cabin in northern Minnesota, and they offered me the use of it; Easter week of 1966, in the company of two friends from the workshop, I made my pilgrimage north, bus to Des Moines, two hours, bus to Minneapolis, four hours, bus to Walker, five hours, and so to the shore of a Minnesota lake. It turned out that this lake was just down the road—a couple of miles—from the lake where Robert Bly had brought James Wright some years before, where both had written a number of the poems that had come to haunt me.

The grocery store nearest the cabin was in the small com-munity of Benedict, and I thought of this visit as my Benedict bull's-eye, a blessing to have come so far to be so close, finding myself shopping at the same grocery store where James Wright and Robert Bly must have picked up their own supplies, their beans and bacon, between poems. My sense of James Wright as a quaffer of nectar was fading already, but this was heady stuff for a poetic young whippersnapper from England, and I still remember the sense of lucky wonder I felt actually to be in the physical area of those poems. Now, all these years later, no longer quite English and a whippersnapper no more, I still shop at that store and have built a home in the woods a mile or two away. James Wright is different for me now, but still I rejoice at the connection. And the English Department of the University of Minnesota in Minneapolis, where James Wright was not happy, where things were often very difficult for him during his six-year stay, where I had adoringly sent him a batch of my early poems in December of 1964, is now my more rather than less happy academic home.

Only a week or two after that first visit north, I heard James Wright for the first time, April 16, 1966, at a reading against the Vietnam War at the University of Chicago, and afterwards asked him to sign my copy of *The Branch Will Not Break*. I enjoyed his reading, the ring of his voice, but he was not the beautiful youth I had pictured in my pre-Raphaelite equation of poetic beauty with pale slenderness. Here is how E. L Doctorow describes him as a student at Kenyon College:

> He was a hulking fellow, not particularly tall but
> built like a wrestler, with sloping shoulders and a size
> eighteen neck. He wore army issue fatigue pants and
> a sweatshirt; this costume he would only vary, as I
> learned over time, with a pair of stiff new overalls.

So much for Rupert Brooke.

And so James Wright became real for me as a person, and it was helpful, and way overdue, for me to start the necessary process of separating him from his poems. But just as I remember my wonderment at finding myself in Benedict, I also feel some amused pleasure in my adolescent imaging of him, pale in his niche in the church of poetry, the sidelight gleaming on him.

Another curious feature of my early feelings about James Wright was my need to rise to his defense when someone attacked his poetry. In 1964, I was incensed when an English magazine published a parody of the composite figure Robert Blight. "MORE BAD NEWS," sneered the parodist, "Old Minnesota Fats is getting thinner every day," and followed this with a piece entitled "Bored with All the Talk of Elections I Slouch Off into the Fields Again, and a Poem Grows from Me Like a Hand or an Ear." I got my Irish up: those English just don't get it, I said to myself in my Surrey vowels, I who was already more than halfway out the door of the island that didn't get it.

On a later occasion, the critic Louis Gallo attacked James Wright in the pages of *The Carleton Miscellany*, mocking "Lying in a Hammock at William Duffy's Farm in Pine Island, Minnesota," and I felt I had to reply. I wrote to the editor to say how selective James Wright was in what he chose to notice in the poem, how, horizontal in a natural temple, he described a mere handful of objects and images. A poem is a sequence of imaginative decisions, after all, and it gives the reader an opportunity to imagine; how visually alive, and how intuitively spaced, the decisions of this poem have always seemed to me, all kinds of room *between* the images for the mind to stretch and leap and wander.

I also wrote about the sound of the poem, about James Wright as a poet of metrical beauty. To my ear, this poem shows a way for free verse to be musical, a pattern of stresses, not regular, but there nonetheless. I love to walk through the poem on the springiness of the stresses: "Over my head, I see the bronze butterfly, / Asleep on the black trunk." That rhythmical pleasure is physical, something to enter again and again and never tire of. Whenever I go to the poem, there it is, waiting. I have always felt that one major way a poem proceeds is on its sound, that the earliest choices of words in a poem offer the poet a proposition of sound, propose an initiative of pattern, which it is the poet's job to carry through to the poem's end. Pattern is, of course, individual for each poet's ear, just as each stringed instrument can have many different tunings. Often poems do not work because nothing is proposed to the ear early on: the words are limp, vibrationless. No suggestion is sent out.

Surely the rhythm of Wright's poem unfolded itself intuitively, un-planned, an opening burst of energy—"Over my head, I see the bronze butterfly"—followed by so much that makes the poem memorable for its sound and meter alone, quite apart from the amazing vividness and mystery of the images. Just in that first line, we hear the majesty of the voiced "s" against the hiss of the unvoiced. Later, we hear a (vowel) reversal of "bronze butterfly" in "comes on." In the final line, we hear the poet's signature of sound—"I have wasted my life": ("I have Jamesed my Wright.") There are so many other seams and echoes of sound; here are some of them: *butterfly* and *trunk; see* and *asleep* and *leaf* and *green* and *ravine* and *between* and *lean* and *evening; bronze* and *butterfly* and *black* and *blowing* and *bells* and *back; over* and *stones* and *floats* and *over* and *home; black* and *trunk* and *back* and *darkens* and *chicken* and *hawk; butterfly* and *distances* and *chicken hawk* and *looking for; green* and *golden; follow* and *field; over* and *blowing* and *shadow* and *empty* and *droppings* and *golden* and *chicken* and *darkens; green* and *down* and *ravine* and *one* and *another* and *afternoon* and *sunlight* and *stones* and *lean* and *darkens* and *on; blaze* and *wasted; asleep* and *ravine* and *between; my* and *I* and *butterfly* and *right* and *light* and *pines* and *life; bronze* and *bells* and *pines* and *droppings* and *blaze* and *as* and *darkens.* The poem is a sequencing, a calling and answering of echoed sounds, that gives pleasure forever. I knew early on that my eye was fascinated with what it saw, but realized only later how much my ear was in love.

How poets delight to repeat, to bring things back, to space them close but intimately apart; delight to send the tongue diving and rising and sliding and rolling, to have the lips gather or widen into the same shapes, over and over. Work of this kind is worship for the mouth as for the ear—everything more musical than it needs to be for information alone, the words themselves blazing up into an aura-language around their mind-meanings. Such a well-made poem "Lying in a Hammock" is. Such a well-made, permanent poem.

And such a joy it is to be *shown* things in poems, provided the showing is as selective as this, as subtle a process as the spacing of sounds. James Wright claimed this poem both was and was not an imitation of the Chinese manner, but he also said: "I can see that Arthur Waley hovers over this poem and guided me, and guided me in responding to what happened that afternoon." The poem certainly has that "endless abundance" that Wright admired in Chinese poetry, which he discussed in an issue of *Ironwood*, as part of a symposium on "Chinese Poetry and the American Imagination." Picking up on something Robert Bly said, James Wright talked about how the kind of space he encountered in translations of Chinese poetry made it possible for him to enter the poem and live there. He went on to praise the Chinese poets for their "capacity to feel . . . an abiding radiance, a tenderness for places and persons and for other living creatures. . . . Time and again these poets can deal with the most commonplace of scenes and occasions, and . . . fill them with clear feeling and with the light of the imagination." I think the sense of imaginative space of his own poem was very much what drew me; there was something distinctive, something that felt American, about the space.

"Lying in a Hammock" was much different from the poems I was raised on, and James talked in an interview about how it made the English critics angry. He could not see why, but I think I do: the piece seems so absurdly relaxed—so much room in it, a breathing painting one can enter over and over. A lot of English critics get mad at Lawrence, too, who was a great poet of place, and also a wanderer, and also a lover of rivers.

Not all parodies of James Wright have made me angry, for parody can also be a form of love. I parodied him, too; many of us did at Iowa, because his style and voice imprinted themselves so strongly on us. There was a worksheet of so-called "Wrighteous" poems, where several workshop poets of the mid and late 1960s had their way with Wright's manner. It includes a piece by Darrell Gray, a poet who died too young, who went up north with me one time, which begins: "A skin of ice is forming on the shallow water. / Far off, across Lake Benedict, the birds are silent. / In their beaks they carry the ashes of elderly picnics, / and the rigid tears of the wheat." Later come these lines—"In Grand Forks, a baby carriage full of minnows / is sold at an auction behind an abandoned feedstore"—and the poem concludes: "Returning to the cabin, I discover that my hands / have been replaced by two magnetic prisms / that can never be used to cook spaghetti again." In a folder in a box somewhere in my garage, where it belongs, is my own parody, "The Brunch Will Not Bake or Whose Corn This Is I Think I Know," a piece not nearly as smart as I thought it was at the time. It ends "I have basted my wife," which is by far the best line, so you can guess at the quality of the rest. I sent it once to Robert Bly, who wrote back to say it had joined the squirming pile of other parodies he had been sent over the years. My favorite parody line from that time at Iowa, also a last line, was written by Ray di Palma: "I have wasted my life, again." Wright is on record as saying, "I love that sort of thing; it was wonderful." He himself contributed to a terrifically funny collective parody of Ransom while he was at Kenyon: "Balls on Joan Whiteside's Stogie."

Perhaps it is time to speculate on the word love in connection with James Wright, why he is acknowledged to be loved by so many of our poets. I call him "My James Wright" to parody the possessiveness of my own early love for his work: I thought he was *mine* somehow, but, of course, he is everyone's. In his *Introduction to Haiku*, Harold Henderson says of Issa, the eighteenth-century Japanese poet, that for all his frailties and the overall sadness of his life, he writes poetry that "opens his soul to us, therefore we love him." To open the soul in poetry means, I think, that the world is generously received into the poem, and reflected there; that the world, and the poet's complex, quarrelling love of it, is everywhere revealed in the writing. The anxious ego does not get to go out and head off the world and bring us back trophy poems, little nuggets of contracted self-expression.

James Wright, who declared himself a Horatian poet by inclination, was not a writer of the inclusiveness of, say, Whitman. But in the best poems, of which there are plenty, there is a generous, tender alertness that reaps an endless abundance of world presence in the text. I think this receptivity is a sign of soul. We find it in such poets as Lawrence or Hikmet or Mistral or Neruda or Cardenal, a swaying when the world sways, a shivering when the world shivers or, as Hikmet says, when a leaf moves at forty days' distance. Such poems are suffused with the world, and none are more so than Wright's final poems, where light and water and creatures and so many inscapes of the world are lovingly observed and let in and given life, so that we know this soul has truly opened itself, and "therefore we love." Well, maybe not certain critics, English and otherwise. Some predecessors gave William Blake a hard time, too, and I've always liked what Edith Sitwell said of him: "Blake was cracked, but that was where the light came in." Wright himself said: "I can still conceive of a poem as being a thing which one can make rather than as a matter of direct expression. . . . It is true that I have written and published a good many poems that do manage to be nothing except direct expression of my own feelings about this and that. I regard those poems as failures." He also said: "It's possible through poetry, I hope, to contribute oneself to the continuity of life, and also to surrender one's own egotism to the larger movement of things."

In 1968, after three years in Iowa City, I went to live out East for three years, and it was then that I got to know James Wright just a little. I heard him at the 92nd Street Y one time, moderating a panel, and also spent one memorable evening with him and his wife Annie when James Tate and I went to their house for dinner. (In a recent letter, Annie recalls the gift of a bottle of wine with a doll's head on it.) I remember him as a friendly, slightly guarded presence, and remember being amazed to hear him quoting paragraphs of Dickens and Hemingway and Ring Lardner by heart. He spoke of the "curse of eidetic imagery" that enabled and obliged him to retain huge quantities of material, prose as well as poetry, so uncannily. I enjoyed those meetings with him and with Annie—there were a couple of other encounters—but I was never close to him and never received a letter from him. Annie kindly wrote me once that James had particularly enjoyed a poem of mine about a toad in Tobago, from a book I had sent them. This was perhaps a little less than I wanted to hear—I suppose I hungered for his approval in some inordinate way—but it was certainly connection of a kind I could never have dreamed of back in England. In this matter of "less," I take comfort from a passage in *The Snow Leopard* by Peter Mathieson, in which the author spends a great deal of money and time traveling to the Himalayas in the hope of glimpsing the legendary snow leopard. Toward the end of the book, after meeting the crippled Lama of the Crystal Monastery, who rejoices in having no choice but to stay where he is, Mathieson walks down the mountain, saying to himself:

> Butter tea and wind pictures, the Crystal Mountain,
> and blue sheep dancing on the snow—it's quite
> enough! Have you seen the snow leopard? No! Isn't
> that wonderful?

In which spirit I say to my younger self: "Did you ever receive James Wright's approval of your poetry? No? Isn't that wonderful!"

The last time I heard his voice was in 1971. I called to tell James and Annie that I was leaving the East Coast and taking a new job. "Where?" asked James. "The University of Minnesota in Minneapolis," I said. Long pause from James. Then, in what seemed to me a quieter tone: "Good luck." And so I moved to the Midwest or, more accurately, to the northern plains, to Minneapolis, and lived for a long time about seven blocks from where James had lived, mostly miserably, on Como Avenue. I used to jog by that little house sometimes and wonder about his life between those walls during those difficult years.

In January of 1980, Robert Bly told me that James was dying. Like many others around that time, I had also received a copy of David Budbill's letter that gave the news of James's illness and relayed Hayden Carruth's suggestion that if ever James's poetry had meant anything to us, now was the time to write and tell him. Immediately, I started work on a long poem, called "Sunflower," into which I poured everything I felt I owed James Wright and loved about his work. It had two epigraphs and it grew to be seven pages long, in six sections. I worked very hard on that poem, obsessively, and, very unusually, read parts of it to students in my classes and over the phone to friends. I am normally much more reticent about works in progress, but this was different: time was short, shockingly short, and I wanted this piece to sum up my indebtedness; I wanted to sing out my love. I had a reading in New York City in March and I decided to read the poem on that occasion. I did read it, the evening of my afternoon visit to James at Mount Sinai Hospital, and I believe I embarrassed myself by doing so because the poem is dreadful—long-winded, willed rather than imagined into being. It has no life of its own. "The merely personal rots," says Yeats, "it must be packed with salt or ice." I'd say there was not enough of either in this epic of protestation of love. One piece of it survives, but on the whole, the urgency of my will was in inverse proportion to the poetic quality of the words I came up with. "I can call spirits from the vasty deep," says Glendower in Henry IV, Part 1. "Why, so can I, or so can any man," replies Hotspur, "But will they come when you call for them?" Here is the surviving part of my poem, the sixth and final section, which I now call "For James Wright":

> I have been jogging,
> and this is the halfway spot
> on the dirt road.
> Before I turn for home
> I stop to look at the pines
> and hear the wind in them.
>
> There are ten—three groups
> of three and four and three—
> and behind them a slope,
> north end of a neighbor's pasture.
>
> Ahead, behind, the dry reeds rustle.
> Weeks from now there will be
> mud and redwing blackbirds here,

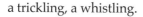

a trickling, a whistling.

Now close my eyes. Now hear the wind,
hissing a little with the needles.
Ten trees. Slowly the branches stir.
My fingers go into the *mudra*,
thumb and forefinger joined,
the other three fingers of each hand
loose, lying open.

Now open my eyes. There are the pines.
Now open my hands
from the *mudra*, let the ten fingers
flutter a moment before me,
then up, up—
over my head I see the butterflies.

Turn then, and begin to run
back down the road, into
the last of the great light.

A few days after my visit to Mt. Sinai, James died. I received
a call in Worcester, Massachusetts, and that night slept over in the
home of friends in Cambridge. I had an early flight the next morn-
ing, and during a very few hours of sleep, I had a dream of unusual
intensity, which I wrote down in my notebook as soon as I woke
up. It seemed to me to be a poem, more or less, and I ended up
calling it "Dream at the Death of James Wright." How strange it is,
but then again perhaps not so strange, that something so brief and
dreamed has, whatever its poetic worth, at least more energy than
the piece I worked on earnestly for weeks and weeks, all choked
up with intention. A little sincerity is a dangerous thing, says Oscar
Wilde, and a great deal of it is absolutely fatal. Here is the poem,
"Dream at the Death of James Wright":

The wind is rolling the buffalo down;
the wind is shining and sharpening the buffalo
and rolling them down.

The sheep have already scattered
toward the forest, sheep are streaming
along the stained edges of the forest.
But the wind is rolling the buffalo down.
We have not built a shelter for them,
we have put up no corral.
They don't know enough to
come together, bind their black fur
together, sit out the storm.
I see one huge one struggling
inside a lantern of grasses.
The wind is rolling the buffalo down,
shining and sharpening them
and rolling them down.

That morning, March 26, 1980, was the day of the service in New York, and I badly wanted to be there. But I had a reading in Evansville, Indiana, before finally heading home. The plane from Boston flew over the Ohio River on its way to Evansville, and I fancied we passed over Wheeling, and so the smudge on the opposite shore had to be Martins Ferry. I sent down a silent prayer.

In September of 1980, six months after James died, I spent a month in China, lecturing on modern and contemporary poetry at Beijing Normal University. I taught some of his poems there, and thought of him often. The Chinese students enjoyed his poems much more than they did the poems of Eliot and Stevens, which they found very demanding. After one particularly strenuous session, in which I had been trying to introduce the main voices of High Modernism, one student sat at his desk mournfully shaking his head: "Too many imaginations," he said. 'Too many imaginations." On one of my last evenings in Beijing, I was a guest at a banquet where, I was told, I would be invited to recite one of my poems. I decided, however, to say a poem by James, who had loved the Chinese poets but had never visited their country. I chose "A Blessing," a luminous poem, one of the windows through which I see the world.

I found that I knew "A Blessing" by heart, without ever having deliberately memorized it. As in "Lying in a Hammock," the images of the poem are striking not only for their beauty and clarity and intimacy but for the judging of space between them. Despite the illusion of sequence in the poem, so much is left out, things that lesser poems tend to fill in. There is a kind of quiet poem that can offer itself to us for the writing if we are attentive, if we don't stride past it whistling loudly, a kind of poem that seems to be whispering: "Over here. Down here." As Jung says, you have to bend to fetch water from the stream. And Meister Eckhart says—James quoted this in a talk he gave in 1967—"Really, to understand anything, including the universe, you have to love it." This love, James went on to say, "is part of your intelligence. It isn't something cut off from your intellect. It is your intellect. And if you don't love it, then you're not paying clear attention to it." One of the great gifts of James Wright is the way he shows us the rewards of that wise and tender attentiveness to everything. He teaches us to receive what the world incessantly offers and withholds or hints at. His is a poetry of presence and absence, speech and silence, side by side.

This is not to say that James Wright is either exclusively receptive or predominantly pastoral. "I'm anti-pastoral," he said in an interview. "I've worked on farms and would never work on another one. I've got up at four o'clock in the morning and shovelled the cow manure out of the barn and bailed away the horse urine. The hell with it." He also said: "Anything can be the location of a poem, as long as the poet is willing to approach that location with the appropriate reverence. Even very ugly places." Many of the images in his work are, of course—as with any writer—based upon interpretation and projection, and the poems would be dead on the page without their contrasts and tensions between the invented and the observed. But what comes through most clearly for me in James Wright's work, taken as a whole, is his honoring of the visible world, his intuitive trust that this attention will reveal, in increments of poems, what can be revealed in no other way. Finally in his work, receptivity is the great wisdom, and there the soul is most present. In one of the final poems, "With the Gift of a Fresh

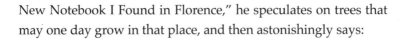

New Notebook I Found in Florence," he speculates on trees that may one day grow in that place, and then astonishingly says:

> I would rather leave them alone, even
> In my imagination, or, better still,
> Leave them to you.

It sometimes seems odd to me that I should have been an Englishman learning to love an American poet in Finland. But James Wright was an American who loved English literature; his honors thesis at Kenyon was on Thomas Hardy, and his doctoral thesis at the University of Washington was on Charles Dickens. And he loved Edward Thomas, his favorite poet—"a holy man, I believe," said James, "a saintly man, without any great public reputation, but one of the secret spirits who help keep us alive."

I want to close by linking James Wright with an English poet I also love with great passion, another whose poems as he approached death—like James's in *This Journey*—took on an unusual beauty. I mean D. H. Lawrence, exile and expatriate, wanderer and lover of rivers, whom I described earlier. Like James, he loved Italy and the south of Europe, and, in fact, he died in the south of France, in Vence, though his ashes are up in the Lobo Canyon in New Mexico. I see many parallels in the way these poets opened to receive the world in their writing, and never more so than toward the end. Both are great poets of the final journey. When the soul is opened, we become connected in ways that underlie all surface distinctions. In the words of my friend John Foley, a composer and a Jesuit, we have a river identity. In his poem "Butterfly," Lawrence writes: "Farewell, farewell, lost soul! / . . . I saw you vanish into air." And in James's poem "Butterfly Fish," he speaks at the end of the fish's other world, "where I cannot see / His secret face." One of the many things to be learned from James Wright, and one of the many reasons to honor him, as I am privileged to do, is the subtle power within the tangible world of the presence of absence.

A talk given at the James Wright Conference,
Martin's Ferry, Ohio, April 1991.

Coda: His Secret Face

I am amazed to hold his notebooks, his papers, in my hands.

I know these kinds of notebooks, these little dimestore, spiral-bound jobs that slip easily into your pocket—the "third companion," as Annie Wright has called them—that went with her and James in their travels. There's nothing out of the ordinary about these sheets of paper, these carbons, these onionskins, this handwriting, this typing. They're not unlike my father's old letters to me, the same texture. I know these crossings out, these scribblings between the lines, these flurries of fresh, wild ideas down the margins, the pooling of alternative phrasings in the spaces below the poems. I know these humble beginnings, these trials-and-errors, these sudden gusts that send you dizzy with possibility, these takings of risks, these why-nots. All familiar. Why not? That's the imagination talking. Why not? Get it all down.

But they're *his*. That's what is so strange. Those poems I first read with something like awe, and certainly with love, almost thirty years ago, in Finland, in England, that high foliage of published pieces I stared up at with wonder, that set me to dreaming of America—here is where they began. I turn page after page and here they are, the roots, the beginnings, all laid out in his hand. But of course. Where else? Unless you could go into his mind, but even the mind of the maker doesn't know what the shape of the thought can be until it releases the syllables onto the page. So the poem starts here, springs from this hillside of the simple notebook or out of the unelectrified 50s typewriter, at all hours of the days and nights of his life, the full spectrum of rages and elations and visions and despairs laid out in language for him to then begin to figure out.

Hooray, he's human. That's what John Berryman thought when he met Yeats once, for the first time, at the Atheneum Club in London. With a shaking hand, the young poet offered the great intimidating Willie a Craven A cigarette, and the great intimidating Willie accepted. Hooray, he's human. Well, I know James Wright was human, and there are several people here today who know it far better than I. I also think it's all right to revere, to be in awe, and when I was in my early 20s and reading his poems for the first time, I was wonderstruck at the beauty of the writing. It revealed the world to me—new aspects, fresh dimensions, of the same world I was coming to know. And now, thirty years later, I am, strange to say it, by a mere handful of months, older than he was ever to be. So that one who was clearly a poetic father is now somehow, by the process of years and my own long apprenticeship, a brother of poetry to me. And yet he will always be the older one.

Reading through the notebooks and papers (by Annie's kind permission), I keep having this image of him down on his knees. Down on his knees in a strong wind while the leaves fly along Como Avenue in 1958 or 1959. Down on his knees in the debris, in the rubble of the syllables, or exploring like a boy the tunnels that run under, smearing onto his face the mud of the words that might be formed into poems. Or, in an imagined elsewhere, climbing, painfully slowly, the steps of the poem, on his knees, like any pilgrim.

I don't think we can be reminded too often, and these notebooks and journals and letters and lists and drafts and revisions and twistings and turnings and dead ends and sudden discoveries enable us to be reminded, whenever we see them, that it is all human. I remember from the exhibit of John Berryman's papers in Wilson Library, in the very same display cases twenty-one years ago, scribbled onto a restaurant menu, the start of a poem I had first admired in its final form in a book. The restaurant is gone; the poem lives. It's easy, of course, to romanticize the author and imagine him or her to be an almost ectoplasmic presence, barely breathing or touching the planet. I did that for sure, once, with James Wright. And it's also all too easy, in the academy today, to remove the writer from the whole enterprise and to privilege the books about writing rather than the books of writing. (But, even

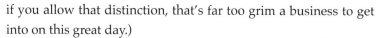

if you allow that distinction, that's far too grim a business to get into on this great day.)

I like how human it is. How his humanness lives in these pages, the endless permutations he was trying out—like a phone number, Auden says, that you're trying to remember, and you check the different possibilities, over and over. Wooing the combinations, as Henry James has it.

He also has a secret face, this artist. In his poem "Butterfly Fish," he writes of the fish's other world, "where I cannot see / His secret face." For all his humanness, he, too, had a secret face that he could never see, that no one can ever see, not in any mirror or in any river. As Paul Eluard writes: "There is another world; it is inside this one." Well, there is a face inside the face. If this face has any texture, it would be like the very delicate membrane that forms the inner part of the eye, the retina, that "sleek and seeing ball," as Hopkins calls it, and the entire surface of it would have the unimaginable optical properties of the eye, so that this hidden retinal face exists in complete attention to the world. (The actual retina, with its more than a hundred million cells, receives light and then sends nerve signals on to the brain; as an image lands upside down on the retina, the signals reaching the brain turn it right side up.)

If the brain is some vast inner solar creative principle, then the secret face, somewhere within and behind the facial mask, serves as its messenger from the outer world. Brain, and soul, will convert what the secret face perceives and sends. And the secret face of James Wright so generously, so tenderly, honors the world in which he led his human life. To read his poems, in either their final published forms or in the versions revealed in the papers and notebooks, is to gain an enlarged sense of what the world can be. Intellect alone, the soul, the heart, the ear, for all their properties, cannot directly decipher the infinitely mysterious world for the benefit of others. They need articulation. Receiving wave after wave of syllables, poems sort, set right side up, pattern, discard and shape what the secret face has alerted them to. What they are able to transform and make permanent is sent back again into the world, as rhythmical language, to the enriching of anyone.

Let me end with something James Wright wrote in his notebook, Tuesday, March 23rd, 1965, at 2:30 in the morning. It shows, I think, one profound use of such a notebook for the artist who keeps it, who is often unaware, at the time of writing, of the value of what has been taken down, what the secret face has perceived. He writes:

> Recently I found a little notebook which I used during late Spring and early Summer of 1962. In my relations with the world, that was a pretty dark period, to put it mildly. And yet—I am astonished at my little notebook of 1962. Here it lies before me now—in fact, I am writing these words on one of its unmarked pages.

> It also happens to contain several completed poems of that year; and three of them were printed in my book The Branch. How very strange! . . . On April 30, 1962, I suddenly wrote "The Jewel"; and it appears in The Branch with very slight changes. Also on April 30, 1962—there it is, right on the next sheet in this very notebook—I wrote, straight out in longhand, without the slightest correction even in ink or punctuation, a little poem, I decline to name, because I know—if I know anything—that it is incomparably the truest & best thing I was ever blessedly lucky enough to write. Then, a couple of pages further, I find three versions of "To the Evening Star," which, like the other two, was later printed in The Branch.

> I suppose the notebook with its poems wasn't enough to save, much less justify, my life . . . But my little notebook was all I had.

Honor to James Wright, and joy at the arrival, and the return, of his writings into our community.

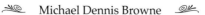 Michael Dennis Browne

*Part of the welcome of the James Wright papers
into the archives at the University of Minnesota,
April 8, 1993.*

Poetry and Hope

Instinct says to begin with a poem, the only poem you will hear this evening which was not written in the twentieth century, since my focus is on the modern and the contemporary. The poem is "Love" by the seventeenth century English poet George Herbert.

Love

Love bade me welcome: yet my soul drew back,
    Guiltie of dust and sinne.
But quick-ey'd Love, observing me grow slack
    From my first entrance in,
Drew nearer to me, sweetly questioning
    If I lack'd anything.

A guest, I answer'd, worthy to be here:
    Love said, you shall be he.
I the unkinde, ungratefull? Ah my deare,
    I cannot look on thee.
Love took my hand, and smiling did reply,
    Who made the eyes but I?

Truth Lord, but I have marr'd them: let my shame
    Go where it doth deserve.
And know you not, says Love, who bore the blame?
    My deare, then I will serve.
You must sit down, sayes Love, and taste my meat:
    So I did sit and eat.

This very beautiful poem by Herbert takes place in the House where Love dwells—the Divine house—to which the guest—humankind—has come. Let me start with an image of the house in which we live, from which we set out to that other place: We live in the carpenter's house. This is where the carpenter returns at night after spending the day working to complete somebody else's house. This is the house in which there are almost as many nails lying about the floor as there are driven into the walls, where there are shapes cut into the walls which will one day be windows whenever the glass can be added. This is the house in which a two-by-four is bracing a partition not yet a permanent part of the structure, where the sub-floor of plywood still waits for the boards of fir or maple or oak to be nailed down over it. It is plywood, not elegant hardwood, that lies under our feet, but for us, and for now, it is the floor. Will it ever be finished, exactly? It doesn't seem likely. And in this way we live in the carpenter's house.

In each of us are many voices. Eight summers ago, I stood near my father's grave in England, praying for help—I was desperate, exhausted: a day or two before, I had been called out of class in Minneapolis to learn that my mother was dangerously ill and had flown to England at six hours' notice. As I stood there in the cemetery, asking for strength, I heard a voice inside which said to me: "Keep up your courage, old son." I had not heard that phrase "old son" in many years; it had been one of my father's familiar affectionate phrases. And I am an old son, I thought, as I would be an old daughter, were I a woman—as though, for example, Shakespeare's Cordelia had survived and was visited later in her life by the voice of the dead Lear. The phrase transformed my day, restored me, stays with me, accompanies my life, causes me to say now how my own voice, the speaking and the poetic, contains not only the voice of a beloved actual father, a dad, Daddy, dead nearly thirty-two years, not only many poetic parents whose writings inspire me, Shakespeare absolutely among them, but also the voice of the archetypal parent, the Word made flesh, whose teachings I was raised on and spent many years away from, only to return to at last. And I am reminded of how in my human contingency, in this unfinishable carpenter's house of a life, I try to respond with my own poetry and my own actions to the deep promises of those other voices.

For the poet, or for this poet, it is not a question of competition with those voices. Rather, it is an exchange, an offering of voice in response to what is being poured unceasingly into my life.

Responding to the voices, echoing them in the form of poetry—that is, writing a real poem—is anyway something I can do only now and then. The rest of the time I live my days without the ability to offer words back toward life. If I manage it, manage a poem, I take for what it is, and try to be grateful; useless to compare oneself with anyone else or agonize over comparisons (not to say one doesn't do it on certain dark nights). For me, it is more a question of finding, to quote David Steindl-Rast, a way of saying *Yes* to that belonging, and in this case, to that belonging of voices, a way of feeling oneself, if only momentarily, one very small weave of voice in the river of all voices. With the phrase—"Keep up your courage, old son"—I was given hope, empowered by a sense of solidarity not only with the spirit of my father but with other voices that have gone before, among them the voices of poetry. These voices remain alive for us, available to us as we struggle, late in this very difficult century, to live lives with the intensity and complexity of hope which life itself deserves. And I was renewed, as I stood on that holy ground, in my determination to be more attentive to all the inner voices, more constant in my practice of the poetry of life.

Tonight, I want to name some poets and poems, and I'll begin with Anna Akhmatova, the great Russian poet. Starting in the 1940s, and into the 1950s, Akhmatova wrote her long poem "Requiem" to express solidarity with thousands of women who were forced to wait daily, for months, outside the walls of a fortress prison in Leningrad for news of their incarcerated loved ones. This was in the 1930s, during the purges orchestrated by Marshal Yezhov, Stalin's head of the NKVD, the Soviet Secret Police. Anna Akhmatova herself was waiting for news of her husband, Nikolai Gumilev. At the beginning of the long poem, she places a paragraph of prose, which she calls INSTEAD OF A PREFACE. (The translation is by Stanley Kunitz and Max Hayward.) She shows herself waiting in line of women outside the prison, all of them desperate for almost any information at all. A tortured-looking woman recognizes the famous poet, and whispers:

"Can you describe this?"
And I said: "I can."
Then something like a smile passed fleetingly over
    what
had once been her face.

How familiar that scene in our century, the torpor and whispering of the desperate. And why should the ruined face smile to hear that the great Akhmatova had the power, and clearly the intention, to describe what she saw and to articulate it as literature? Because politics, as the American poet Charles Olson has said, is eyes. And poetry is eyes, one of the most courageous and consistent of witnesses available in our time. Those eyes watch; they record. And poetry is mouths, not merely the poet's but the mouths of those who have been silent until now, and it gives voice to the voiceless; it speaks truth to power, as the Quakers say (and as Grace Paley records it). In speaking that truth, poetry empowers both speaker and listener, both writer and reader. Sometimes, it almost unthinkably empowers the writer, so that a courage remote to Akhmatova, in prospect, at the beginning of her poem, begins to suggest itself, painfully, as her own words unroll, and, subsequently, a transformation occurs. Susan Griffin, a contemporary American writer, describes the process this way:

Each time I write, each time the authentic words
break through, I am changed. The older order that
I was collapses and dies. I lose control. I do not
know what words will appear on the page. I follow
language. I follow the sound of the words, and I am
surprised and transformed by what I record.

What is generated, by means of the poem itself, is a sense of resolve which grasps the poet—and there is all the difference in the world, as someone once said, between grasping something and being grasped *by* it. The result is that we are able, reader and writer, to re-dedicate ourselves to the task at hand with a re-charged energy of attitude, able to leave the microcosmic, rhythmical world of the poem and re-enter the world around it, inclined, either once again or for the first time ever, to "ask for great things," as Joachim Jeremias says in his essay on the Lord's Prayer. The verbal ritual of the poem re-connects us to our lost purposes, reminds us of the size of the enterprise on which we are all embarked. The business of poetry, says Charles Baudelaire, is to make us see how large and poetic we are in our boots and hats and ties.

By means of her own words, Anna Akhmatova's terror becomes fused with the terrors of many others, on whose behalf, as well as her own, she speaks, and it is alchemized, over the course of the poem, into a rare courage. She is changed forever by her own utterance. Early in the poem, she speaks nostalgically about the town where she was raised, where the great poet Pushkin was also born; at the end of the poem, she rejects the thought of returning there, even in the form of a statue after her death. Why should that be? Because then she would be too far removed from the scene of her solidarity with the other women:

> Because even in blissful death I fear
> to lose the clangor of the Black Marias,
>
> to lose the banging of that odious gate
> and the old crone howling like a wounded beast.

This exceptional resonance of vision, coming from a writer whose work could not be published in her home country for forty years, whose poems survived only by being committed to memory by certain friends, is one of the many causes for hope for poetry in this century.

Another great European poet, Czeslaw Milosz, has written about horrifying events in Poland during the German occupation of World War II, less than ten years after the purges of which Akhmatova wrote. In one of the essays in his book *The Witness of Poetry*, Milosz says that when literature bore witness to these events, "a peculiar fusion of the individual and the historical took place, which means that the events burdening a whole community are perceived by a poet as touching him in a most personal manner. Then poetry is no longer alienated." In other words, the poet takes public tragedies personally, takes the fates of so-called others absolutely personally. Then poetry becomes one with the soul of the people. This echoes what Shelley says of the poet in his *Defence of Poetry*: "the pains and pleasures of his species must become his own." Milosz also asserts that for all the terrors of our time, the poet lives unconsciously on hope; this speculation comes to us from a writer well acquainted with the agonies of war, of enemy occupation, of torture and reprisal, of exile.

What is this hope of poetry? It is, for one thing, participation in a world at once unbelievably heart-breaking and inexhaustibly fertile (it seems impossible to avoid paradox when we speak either of the world or the imagination). It is to try daily, with each breath, to "heal reality with reality," in the words of the Israeli poet Yehuda Amichai, himself a veteran of five wars. What time or excuse for a self-absorbed mourning of one's own separate life is there when one is being borne "on great winds across the sky," in the words of an Ojibwe poem? History, worldly and spiritual, requires our participation.

Another poet of Akhmatova's stature, Nazim Hikmet, the revolutionary Turkish poet, a Marxist, who died in exile in Moscow in 1963, again and again shows in his poetry an unquenchable love of the world and an astonishing sense of connection with those who struggle for justice and who suffer. Hikmet had a heart condition, which eventually killed him, and in his poem "Angina Pectoris," he writes that while half his heart is in his physical body, half is in China with the army, and "every morning, doctor, at sunrise my heart is shot in Greece." Hikmet spent much of his life in prison because of his revolutionary activities; in another poem, "Some Advice to Those Who Will Serve Time in Prison," he writes of shivering inside jail "when outside, at forty day's distance, a leaf moves."

The empathy to be found in Hikmet's poetry has had a large effect on my own life and writing. The empathy is authentic;

once you encounter it, there is no going back from it. It makes its mark. "All changed," wrote Yeats at the time of the Easter Rising in Ireland in 1916, "changed utterly: / A terrible beauty is born." What does Gabriela Mistral, the great Chilean poet, call it? "The wound of love inflicted on us by things." Terrible beauty, wound of love—the hope of poetry is never found too far from paradox. And through poets such as Yeats, Mistral, Pablo Neruda, D. H. Lawrence, or contemporaries such as Wendy Rose, Audre Lorde, Ernesto Cardenal, Denise Levertov, June Jordan, the voices of poetry have risen to the occasion of this harsh century time after time, poem after poem, to deliver both condemnation and praise with all the music of language and energy of image they can summon. The hope of poetry is in such voices, and in the rhythms in which they are presented to us, which ride into the heart and take up residence there. Cell by cell, they work their transformations upon us; gradually they accumulate into the way we see the world and the way we act in the world.

In the case of Hikmet, you can certainly call his vision humanist, call it secular, in the sense that there is no eschatological comfort, and you can certainly call it heroic, epic, something almost of a modern secular scripture; it constitutes a dedication of an unusual clarity to the purely human. In his poem "On a Journey" (all the translations are by Randy Blasing and Mutlu Konuk), Hikmet tells us of the inevitable disasters of life, and ends by saying, "Yet if I could / start this journey over again, / I would. And in yet another remarkable poem, "On Living," he says " you have to feel this sorrow now, / for the world must be loved this much / if you're going to say 'I lived.'"

Hikmet makes great demands on us in his insistence that we grieve and love the world with such an immediate intensity. It's tempting to want to look away from the world, with its daily menu of horrors, and not try to reconcile the polarities of grief and love with the radiance which shines in these poems, but the writers I most admire re-dedicate themselves, poem by poem, to the work at hand, "the real work," as Gary Snyder calls it. One cannot turn away: however terrible the prospect, "I am supposed to look," as Linda Gregg writes in her poem "There She Is."

And when the poem succeeds, what it is that happens? It has been said that a good poem about something is always also about something else, and what happens, often, in the convincing poem, is that it generates its true subject, and "the poem behind the poem" appears, often to the surprise, even astonishment, of the writer. A poem can often begin as a dialogue with one's own unbelief—"I believe, help Thou my unbelief"—but it does not always end there. According to A. E. Housman, the poet's job is to "harmonize the sadness of the world." It's a magnificent phrase from one of our saddest poets; it suggests that other voices are brought in to join with the single voice; the collective sound is choral, larger. I might also add that the poet's job is also to remind us of possibilities, to revive the subsided vision in us, so that we can re-kindle the fire, as in the great liturgy of the Easter vigil, so that we can breathe onto the waters of life new breath.

In Richard Wilbur's poem "The Writer," a successful, middle-aged poet learns hugely from his own complacency and is, by the end of his poem, "changed utterly." (Love, says the same poet in another poem, "calls us to the things of the world." This poem begins with a room in a house in Massachusetts but ends in the world at large.

It is always a matter, my darling,
Of life or death, as I had forgotten. I wish
What I wished you before, but harder.

Whenever I hear those final lines, when they occur to me in difficult times, I feel stirred and renewed. It must be that they are telling me—are telling us—something necessary, something we can never tire of, that we need to keep hearing.

The same holds true for a stirring poem by Sharon Olds, "Prayer During a Time My Son Is Having Seizures," in which the poet begins as "a woman without belief," a helpless implorer, and ends resolute and determined. Sharon Olds talked once, on a classroom visit, about her desire to write poems "on the side of life," and there is a way in which poems echo the prodigal journey, or they take up their story at the point where the prodigal unbelief begins an attempt to return to the source, to the side of life, away from death and back toward the original condition of belief. While the voice in me appeared unbidden as I stood dispirited and in tears near the ruins of my father's body, in the poem we generate through acts of language the soul that is within us, the one who knows that it is always a matter of life and death, as Wilbur says in the conclusion to his poem. In her poem, Sharon Olds manages to return to a loving faculty centered within herself, one which sees what is possible, and which she, like Wilbur, had forgotten.

Some of the details in that shattering and ultimately hopeful poem are of a kind you might not have expected to find in poetry till fairly recently, until this century, more or less, and I want to say something now about hope in connection with a paradox which lies at the heart of poetry. Rilke, the German poet, tells us, in his poem "The Man Watching," that what we fight with in our lives is small; at the same time, what is fighting with us is great. Who is it fighting with us, below our consciousness, as we grapple with our trivial preoccupations? It is larger beings, says Rilke, angels, who are wrestling with us. When we win, it's with small things, he says, and "the triumph itself makes us small." What does he recommend? That we let go our little obsessions and allow our-selves to be defeated, decisively, by "constantly greater beings" (the translation is by Robert Bly). But here is the paradox: in the ninth "Duino Elegy," the same poet Rilke advises us against writing large, writing about the cosmos—we human beings are amateurs there, he says: the cosmos is the province of the angels; let *them* use the big words. But if such an angel were to come to earth, says Rilke, then what we should do is show our visitor things we know about—the rope-maker in the open market, for example, or the thrower of pots, centering the clay with wet, stained hands. Then we would truly behold some angelic amazement. These are the things we know, we who are not angels, on earth our home, and this is where we establish our vision. If the goal of art is transformation, then the goal is to end where we began and "see it for the first time," in Eliot's phrase, in all its ordinariness and miraculousness. Nothing special, as they say in Zen.

Here is one chief hope of poetry—and one deep joy—its attentiveness to the offered world, to the phenomena of the visible and natural universe, all the mysteries of surface and mass and texture and light. All these beings and objects have their own consciousness, their own news for us. When D. H. Lawrence, the expatriate English writer, saw the New Mexico landscape for the first time, he wrote: "The moment I saw the brilliant, proud morning shine high above the deserts of Santa Fe, something stood still in my soul and I started to attend." His ashes now lie in that ground. The hope of poetry is in attentiveness. If we attend to the act of breathing, for example, that familiar, infinitely mysterious act, we become more aware of the entire breathing universe around us; then we have the chance to become what Charlotte Joko Beck, in her book *Everyday Zen*, calls "a bigger container." Everything is to be noticed; nothing is too humble as a source of revelation. "And if a sparrow come before my window," says Keats, "I take part in its existence and peck about at the gravel." Poets are right to be wary of abstraction—*abtrahere*, to pull away from—because it can draw us too far away from the numinous immediacy of the things around us. Poetry relishes the things and attends to them.

On this issue, poet and theologian are not far apart. Karl Rahner writes that though love "demands God himself," yet "it must be mediated by the events of every day, actualized across the whole gamut of the realities of one's life." Human beings, says Rahner, "would betray their divine hope if they repudiated their earthly task." We must attend to the offered world because it, not the cosmos beyond, is where we are to generate our destiny. Where would our poems be if we attempted to by-pass the world and the moment—what Rabbi Abraham Joshua Heschel calls "the herenow."—to compete with the angels whose province is the cosmos? How real would they be if we did not trust the world as the container of the soul? Images are our earthly task; through them we can inquire freshly, with each poem, not only, in James Hillman's words, "what happened today?" but what "happened to the soul today?" The soul needs the created world for its expression.

They stay small physically, of course, poems, a mere handful of lines at a time, even the so-called long ones. But just as a single first human cell can contain all the evidence needed to unfold one entire human life—I read once that the genetic information contained within that first cell would amount to seven thousand pages in a book as we know it—so the microcosm of the poem can suggest something of the size and infinite subtlety of our whole human enterprise. "Eternity," says William Blake, "is in love with the productions of time." And so he writes of seeing the world in a grain of sand, heaven in a wild flower. What was the Buddha's sermon? He held up a flower. Christ himself teaches us with tangible parables, which trust the things around us to evoke things within and beyond us, landscapes of the soul and the spirit. The hope of poetry is in our attention to the world in which correspondences between the seen and unseen lie all around us.

I talk of flowers. One of the responsibilities of the poet today, according to an essay by Robert Pinsky, *Responsibilities of the Poet*, is to resist our culture's subtle enforcement of unconscious ideas about what is and what is not poetic, what it is our business to attend to. For example, the notion that to write about flowers is acceptable, but politics is unpoetic. Try telling that to an artist in any embattled culture, such as Nicaragua or China—or the United States. In other words, the poet embraces all possible subject matter, locates and names the poetry in everything. The hope of poetry is also in the liberation of subject matter, and revelation is at hand in often unlikely places, places the world at large, domination systems, would judge unsuitable.

Elizabeth Bishop's poem "Filling Station" would be just one example of the kind of subject matter I have in mind. At its end, such a revelation springs out of the world of the service station she brilliantly conjures through several stanzas—"Somebody loves us all." But poetry can do this, again and again, in its attentiveness to what is near at hand. The same poet has written entirely tougher, grittier poems when other contexts called them from her, and I believe our poems should have "fidelity to experience," as Denise Levertov calls it, should reflect the range of our lives: When we celebrate, let our poems radiate that celebration; when we grieve, let the grief be fully alive in our words. A friend told me once in college—"Michael, you won't move people with your sorrows, you'll move them with their own"—and what I have been learning over years of writing is that attention to lives other than mine, itself a good, can also bring discoveries about your own self which would never shown themselves in any other way.

I'll talk now a little about my own poetry, and my own hope, and try to describe my evolving practice. A main amazement to me, as I travel toward a deeper sense of the meaning of a life of faith as an artist might live it, is the central fact of the Incarnation. "The Word was made flesh and dwelt among us." Emily Dickinson wrote once that she knew when she was hearing poetry because it felt as if the top of her head were being taken off. For myself, there are times when the news of the Incarnation, the very notion of it, causes me to shiver in every cell in my body. It is not so unlike the sensation I experience when I look at my children, those dreams made flesh, vessels of the spirit, whom I am privileged to nourish in this life. With the example of Christ, we carry about with us the most exquisite, agonizing emblem of participation in humankind.

In Elie Wiesel's book *Night*, when the child is hung in the concentration camp, a slow, dreadful hanging, someone calls out: "Where is God? Where is he? Where is God now?" And watching the child taking a long long time to die on the end of a rope, Wiesel hears a voice within, which says: "Where is He? Here He is—He is hanging here on this gallows." With the Incarnation in mind, heart, soul, what choice do we have but to undergo, in the words of Thomas Merton, "the penance of getting to know the nightmare cruelty of the modern world, not this time from any unconscious masochistic motive, but in order to begin the heartbreaking task of trying to evolve a new pattern"? If Christ is, to use Pascal's revolutionary phrase, "in agony till the end of time," how should we finish our own house? How should the temple not stand incomplete "until all are housed in dignity"? If Christ remains our God-with-us, in a condition of at-one-ment with us as we celebrate and grieve, how should we consider ourselves immune either from sacrifice or from hope? The phrase "Keep up your courage, old son," which I heard inside as I stood in the cemetery in England, put my responsibility to me very plainly. I left that place renewed in my determination to operate as clearly as I can, to mediate with whatever voice I have between those who went before, those who are living now, among them my children, everyone's children, and those yet to live, among them my children's children, everyone's children's children.

The fate of the children, to whom we will be leaving this world, involves me now in ways I could never have anticipated in my earlier years. Here are a few lines from a poem I wrote in May 1990 on the occasion of the twentieth anniversary of the massacre of students at Kent State, and read a few hundred yards from where the students had been shot on the campus of Kent State. About halfway through the poem, I talk directly to the four slain students, and I ask them:

> Allison, Jeffrey, Sandra, William,
> what to say to them, the children,
> in your name, in our voices
> our imagined voices feed?
> . . . the children,
> those worlds expecting that seeds
> of the believing, not the despairing life,
> be sown in them.

I have come to believe irrevocably in the necessity of the believing life—I can't say my temperament always cooperates with me in this endeavor—and I try to work to become a "bigger container," to keep myself aimed toward hope, which remains unseen.

(Paul tells us that the hope that can be seen is not hope. Buddhism has a tougher phrase—"If you meet the Buddha on the road, kill him.") I try also to keep myself tuned to that hope, to the frequency of those voices, though reception is never certain. And which are the voices, I ask myself daily, which nourish us? And which are the voices that must be replied to? Voices which drag us down?

I stay aimed toward hope, I remind myself daily, because of the Incarnation, and because we have been promised—most astonishingly promised. We have been told that whatever the tensions and horrors we must live through, all shall (ultimately) be well. We have been told that if we ask, we will receive, that if we knock it will be opened to us, that eye has not seen, nor ear heard, neither has it entered into our hearts what things await us. All these are images of the purest poetry I know, and they stir me as no other images do because of their source and because of the grandeur of their claims. "Behold, I am with you all days," we have been told. We have been told there is a kingdom within, that in a world which daily crucifies, we are already redeemed, already holy. How precious are we to the eternal source—we "the unkind, the ungrateful," as George Herbert calls himself and us—as we participate in this world? We have been told (Luke 12): "Are not five sparrows sold for two pennies? And not one of them is forgotten before God. Why, even the hairs of your head are all numbered. Fear not; you are of more value than many sparrows."

The main epigraph for the book I am writing now, a fifth collection of poems, is that passage. The question I ask myself daily is—how are we to reconcile the conditions of the world, as we observe them with our literal eyes, with the promises that have been made to us? I *try* to live that question. Don't we shiver daily, as sparrows shiver, in the blasts of unbelief? I have already suggested that a poem often begins out of an impulse to set unbelief in dialogue with other possibilities, but it is folly to enter the poem predicting any kind of facile resolution. Rather, we learn to live in the spaces between unbelief and belief, so deathly afraid of life at times, at others so wordlessly grateful. The world will not come to any easy closure. And we must live its questions. "The world is building," says Pierre Teilhard de Chardin, "the world is an immense groping." Teilhard de Chardin was a great lover of the world of matter as well as of the world promised by the resurrection; "I bless you, matter, and you I acclaim," he says. Who would not find hope in such a notion, that we are partners, carpenters all, in the building of the world?

One of the prayers I was raised on describes this world as a vale of tears, but what is it John Keats calls the world? A vale of soul-making, said the English poet, dead of consumption at twenty-five. When the surgeon opened up Keats' lifeless body, he found the lungs almost entirely destroyed and expressed amazement that Keats had lasted so long and burned with such a flame. I take great courage from the very young Keats. How much he loved life from out of his ravaged body! How much hope he lived by.

The image I began with, the carpenter's house, I offer you one last time as a symbolic image of the imperfections and incompletions we necessarily live among and must embrace—our own very raw materials. They are not always impressive, these lives of ours, these bodies, these plans, these worlds, something makeshift about them, never or rarely quite what we had in mind, and we know they do not abide. Everything moves, moves on, moves by, moves away—not just the clouds, the rivers, but we, the generations. These lives are what we have, who we are; we live with that paradox of the great intentions, the great promises, and, on the other hand, the all-too-fallible materials. But they were not too humble for our Emmanuel. And so we dedicate ourselves to the work we have to do.

Fifteen months ago, I attended a ceremony on Holy Hill in Berkeley which commemorated the Jesuit priests martyred, together with their housekeeper and her daughter, in El Salvador, and what we heard at that assembly, a message brought by activists from El Salvador, and echoed by activists in the community, was the familiar and necessary one: *Don't mourn them—imitate their lives. And organize.* Poetry participates in that imitating, poetry participates in that organizing. (Martyr means witness.) It offers back to life, in that passionate exchange Rosemary Haughton speaks of in her book *The Passionate God*, soberly hopeful opposition to injustice and hopeful praise both of the given world and the immense redemption which is a gift beyond our understanding.

To finish, I'll read you four of my poems. The first, "Hide and Go Seek," was written after a visit to England some fourteen years ago. I see my nieces and nephews "over the water" rarely enough, and this particular occasion had a wild and loving energy to it, which I have tried to capture.

Hide and Go Seek

for Lisa

I count to fifty.
Then I appear at the French window;
in my hand, the three-flame candelabrum.
The children have run to hide in my sister's garden.
It is March, damp dark, that English dark I left.

I make the monster sound.
I give the groan they long to hear, and fear.
I can almost feel their shivering out there.

Then I begin to move.
I lurch stiff-legged. I sway.
I am the Mud Man, come
still smeared from his swamp,
I am something extinct
with my rotting fingers,
I am the slimy thing from the sea
who leaks after them on feet
horribly like the human hand, but heavier.
I am he no longer afraid of fire,
who points these prongs of flame to find them.
I need some blood.
I need to catch me some family flesh
and chew it down to the bone.

Appalled, they hurtle all over,
the nephews, the nieces,
they scatter, they stream
round Fran and Angela's garden,
desperate scared, mad scared—
who let this thing loose in England?—
run! run!—
the Bogey Man, the Bog Beast—
run! run!

Roaring, reaching out,
again and again I miss them,
so slow I am,
so sleepy with my swampy blood,
miss them just enough to freshen their fear,
to send them screaming further
into the dark,
out behind the beanpoles,
behind the compost,
behind the favorite tree that is now
metal to the touch.
I hear, I hear the panting.

And—it is enough. Now it is done.
Now I raise the candles to show
my friendlier face—I am Michael again,
the almost American uncle,
and I call to them: All in, All in.
Together we go toward the house
through the garden that is their again,
laughing, still thrilled with our fright.
And Damien, my godson, four,
that boy of light I sought in the dark,
shouts: "I'm bigger than myself!"

Whoever the seekers, children,
whoever will chase you,
if inside you, if behind you,
may they miss, I pray it,

may they not touch,
may you make it
past such grasping and reach the house
as now together we do,
where people are waiting who love us
and from darkness welcome us.
O mystery of family. O darkness. O house.
I pray it: All in. All in.

There's quite a high drama in that poem, and a monster who alarmed the children to what I had to calculate were acceptable levels. With such games, we help them rehearse the world.

In this next poem, "Watering," there is no such drama. The poem takes place in a very different kind of garden—a small vegetable and flower garden by a cabin in the north woods—and I can say that I learned something from it. I learned that my compassion is too shallow, too selective, too inconsistent, that whatever nurturing I may have done so far is too little in the face of what the world needs, what the "voices of the soil," what the multiplying "mouths of the earth," require. I also learned, I think, or was reminded, that the kind of pouring out of one's life that is proposed in the poem can only be accomplished, if at all, by means of grace, by an inpouring of the spirit whose breath is life. Part of the hope I feel is that this awareness I came to was there all the while for me to uncover, there in the ancient promise that if you lose your life, you will find it. And part of the hope for me, in terms of the attentiveness and "acclaiming of matter" I have been talking about too light, is that this is also a poem about gardening, and the water is real. It was, by the way, written to be set to music by John Foley S.J., a wonderful composer and spiritual teacher, with whom I have had the joy of collaborating on a musical version of the gospel of Luke, called *As a River of Light*. This poem is the last in a sequence of six poems which John set as a song cycle about three years ago.

Watering

It is a timid rain, that leaves

the topsoil moist.
Go down an inch or two,
and it is dust.

So you must drench and drench,
mimicking the heaven that cannot,
it seems, leave earth alone,
as if heaven itself took form
to stand there, watering.

When is it enough? For all
you can spill, more will appear
to be poured through you.
All the voices of the soil
require your pouring, require
such a rain as you
had not ever thought
to let fall. Many, multiplying
are the mouths of the earth.

Can dry ground dream of rain?
What hope for the ground
without what it cannot dream of?
Then you must stand and stand
until all dreams of dust
are done, until
all you are is rain.

It can be dangerous, writing poems—sometimes the statement
the poem makes sets a standard it can be just a little hard to live up
to! But I should say that I try not to live so much by standards as by
images, and images have an affect, a dynamic, which no abstract
statement can match. And from images, even just occasionally my
own, I can draw strength.

I want to end with the first and last poems in my new book,
You Won't Remember This. In this book I have set my fears and pre-
monitions in dialogue with my hope. I am aware that "perfect love
casts out fear"; the struggle for me, in which my writing plays a
main part, is to try to clear the space in myself in which that love

can take root and grow. Breathing, meditation, the practice of the presence of God, as Brother Lawrence calls it, all contribute to the work of clearing. I try to say *Yes* to that love, *Yes* to the voices, *Yes* to that belonging, *Yes* to asking for great things. The hope of poetry is in dialogue with what fearfully occupies and preoccupies us, and in our naming of it, in living out the tensions of the dialogue, in our coming to praise the immensity of all we have been given.

The first poem is called "Mengele" and has a monster in it very different from the playful one of "Hide and Go Seek." Wilfred Owen, the English poet killed at the end of World War I, said that poets must warn; this poem speaks in a warning voice. It was written after I read in the paper of the discovery of the bones of Joseph Mengele, the so-called Angel of Death of the concentration camps, in Brazil in 1985. The newspaper report suggested that this discovery closed the Mengele chapter. The imagination protests such simplicities and this poem was my spontaneous attempt to "speak truth to power."

Mengele

Don't tell me about the bones of Mengele,
the bones are alive and well.
Don't think to thrill me with tales
of the drowned bones uncovered,
the bones are alive and well
inside the sleeves of a suit this day
and carving out the figures of a fat check
or accepting a ribbon with the ceremonial scissors
or holding the head of a child.
I tell you, the bones are alive and well.

Don't expect me to get excited
concerning the skull of Mengele,
the skull is alive and well,
the skull is asquirm with schemes this day
and low words are leaving it at this moment
and other skulls are nodding at what they hear,
seated about the world table;

I tell you, the skull is alive and well.

Don't bother showing me pictures
of the remains of Mengele,
the remains are alive and well
and simmering in our rivers
or climbing into our houses out of the ground
where they will not be confined
or sliding inside the rain
out of the summer air, oh yes,
the remains are even there, I tell you,
are alive, are well, are everywhere.

Part of the hope of poetry, as I have tried to show, is in its insistence on warning, on its witness of injustice and oppression. And part of the hope is in the joy and sense of blessedness which, on occasion, unaccountably, flood our lives. At the end of the book, and of this talk, I offer you a direct contrast to what you just heard, a poem called "Evensong," a very quiet piece, which has to do with a drive along dirt roads in the north woods; this was in April, nearly four years ago, at day's end, and my two children were in their seats behind me. The "he" of the poem is my son Peter, now eight, and he gets to speak in this poem because, in fact, he said things, already at four-and-a-half years being very fond of using words. The "she" of the poem, strapped into a car seat, is my daughter Mary, now aged five, and she doesn't get to talk in this poem because she was only nine months old at the time; I think she was merely saving her strength for the floods of words she now delivers daily into our lives so blessed by the gift of these new beings. Here is the poem:

Evensong

"There he is" he learns to say
when we glimpse the great sun burning down
toward the hill, and "There she is"
when we spot the pale, enormous moon
floating low above the pines;

and over and over, swiveling his head,
he says it as I drive them both,
daughter and son, around the roads
until they sleep, so I can have
dinner and an hour alone with their mother.

Ahead in the shadows, two deer.
A little further, metal abandoned
in somebody's yard, auto parts
and ancient appliances, that later
the moon will make into something
that same skilled stranger keeping us
company beyond the branches.

He wants to know why they share the sky,
and all I can tell him is it's a secret
we have to guess at as we go;
and "There he is" he says once more
as the hill prepares to swallow fire,
and "There she is" as she climbs the air,
and murmurs and murmurs until he sleeps
(and she already is sleeping).

*College of Saint Benedict, St Joseph,
Minnesota, February 1992.*

Listening

I want to talk to you today about the importance of listening for the poet. In an article in a recent issue of *The New Yorker*, written by the American poet and translator Alistair Reid about the British poet Robert Graves, Reid had this to say about Graves in later age:

> The stance he struck became ever more adamant,
> even shrill. I think he had stopped listening—to those
> close to him, to his own commonsense self, even to
> his own misgivings.

"He had stopped listening." Whether or not that is a fair assessment of Graves, I know from personal experience, as a writer, teacher, husband, father, friend, some of the consequences of stopping listening. Today, of course, I want to concentrate on poetry.

As a teacher of poetry, in recent years I have found myself suggesting to people I work with, at any level of experience, from beginning to advanced, that they record one poem a week, say, a poem by a living poet—just talk into the microphone of a small portable recorder in a relaxed, natural voice, I suggest, or, if you have a partner or friend whose voice you enjoy, have that person record it for you. Then listen to the poem half-a-dozen times during the week, as you drive or bike or jog or walk or do the dishes. Let the sounds and sequences of the poems sink into you.

A poem is a sequence of very intimate linguistic decisions; I believe we can all learn from living on more intimate terms with its sounds. Denise Levertov calls a poem "a sonic structure." Even if its music is a very casual, colloquial one, as in, say, William Carlos Williams, rather than some grand, high modernist music—Yeats, for example—still, we need to let the poem into our inner ear, into our heart and soul. If you were to do this weekly recording and listening beginning today, I tell my students, when we met in this room one year from now, you would then have circulating in you fifty-two texts which presently you do not possess. They would have become a part of you. Someone like myself is never your best teacher, I say, though people like myself can help; your best teacher is always your own coming to poetry, your coming to love, by listening, a range of writings which use language as fully as possible to take the measure of human consciousness and human experience.

I'm not that good a listener. But I believe I'm getting better; I'm working at it. Recently, I've written a couple of book reviews, and in each case I first recorded the collection of poems—it took about an hour and a half—and then listened to it three or four times before I wrote the review. I felt I knew the voice of the poems better, knew the span of the book better, by that listening. Sharon Olds, on a classroom visit once, talked about a Muriel Rukeyser workshop in which the dozen or so writers discussed a poem on a worksheet only after each member of the group had read it out loud in turn. That may be extreme, and it wouldn't be feasible in a larger group, but in some ways it also sounds ideal. You hear the poem, over and over. That's a sequence of thoughts and feelings you begin to know. It sinks in. It inhabits you, and even perhaps, if you are lucky, comes to haunt you.

Sharon Olds also described another Muriel Rukeyser class—I think I am remembering this right—in which, after one reading out loud of Gerard Manley Hopkins' poem "Pied Beauty," the group recreated the poem from memory. Someone had the first line, someone the first half of the second, someone the second half of the fourth line, and so on. Gradually and finally, they put it together on the blackboard. There were probably some disagreements along the way, such as—"Surely that's not right . . . no, that doesn't sound like it . . . that's not how it goes . . . wasn't there? . . ." and so on—but finally the piece was assembled as the poet had written it. This is a great way to get down inside a poem and its patterning.

And I remember an experience from a conference in St Petersburg, Florida, a couple of years ago, when several of the conference faculty were giving a brief reading after a banquet. When it came to her turn, Toi Dericotte recited the poem which begins: "There was a man of double deed / Who sowed a garden full of seed"—it consists of about a dozen such rhyming couplets—and then challenged all of us, students and faculty, to recreate it on the spot. No, no, no, we couldn't possibly manage that, we all said. With surprisingly little struggle, we *did* manage it. It's a very catchy piece, of course, very mnemonic with its bright rhymes, but still, we were impressed!

I think we need to listen more to poems. Into poems. To honor their oral aspect. And today, I want to pay homage to the act and the art of listening. Listening as gift. Listening as refreshment. Listening as renewal. Listening as reciprocity. Listening as tenderness of attention toward the strung moments of someone else's rhythmical story—a story never told before quite like this, with quite these words. Listening as blessing, the moment-by-moment blessing of attentiveness to what another is saying and singing, to the intimacy of what someone else has brought together in language. Freud writes of the basic criteria for mental health as being the ability to work and to love; I'd like to add to that the ability to bless—a faculty related, of course, to love. To be able to bless. Right listening as the blessing of attentiveness.

To listen, to be attentive, we have to empty ourselves. I'm not necessarily good at this either; I have to practice it. In his book *The Miracle of Mindfulness*, the Vietnamese monk Thich Nhat Hanh suggests that when we drink a cup of tea, let that cup be the axle on which the world is turning. Let us be doing only that. And you may know the story of the western professor of philosophy who traveled east, traveled many days, to learn the lessons of life from a certain wise one in the mountains. When he had found the guru, he engaged him in conversation, was very animated, asked lots of questions, talked and talked and talked. When tea was served, the host poured for his guest, and he kept pouring even after the cup was filled; tea went all over the floor and down the steps. There was no room in the guest, the host was implying, for whatever he himself might have to offer. The professor was too full—too filled up with what he knew or thought he knew. Too many agendas. Listening requires emptying. If we are to let the sounds in, we have to learn to be empty in order that we may be filled. We need to practice emptying.

When we make a poem, of course, we are listening to the language, listening into it, all its possibilities. It's the poet's job to listen. Let's ask ourselves—how alive, how alert are we, as we play with the permutations of syllables, as we "woo the combinations," as Henry James has it? With each poem, we have to learn all over again how to listen. "The living poets carry the language forward," says Elizabeth Drew. How can we carry it forward if we don't listen to what it has already done? That is the renewal which listening can bring. We think we know how—we have been listening all our lives, right? We have also been talking all our lives, using words, but is that ever a guarantee that we can sit down and create the living structure of sounds we call a poem? What intensity of attentiveness, what relaxed intensity of attentiveness, do we have to bring to bear in the making of a poem?

Each occasion of our lives requires fresh responses of behavior from us. Each occasion of poetry requires fresh responses, fresh patterns of language, from us. We can unload onto a new situation all the old learned responses or we can attend to this moment, this occasion, by listening to what it asks of us, by improvising, as Alfred Alvarez once wrote of Lawrence's poems, "at the full pitch" of our intelligence. It's a question of proportion, naturally; we need the skills we have, the skills we have acquired—what does Pope say?—"as those move easiest who have learned to dance"—but we need the freshness of response which characterizes the surprise of true poems.

Charlotte Joko Beck, in her book *Everyday Zen*, writes of being a piano major at Oberlin Conservatory, starting out as already a "very good" player but encountering a teacher who said "No" to her each time she played the five notes he had first played; this went on for months, and finally, one day, the teacher said "Good." "What had happened?" she asked herself. "Finally, I had learned

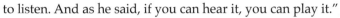

to listen. And as he said, if you can hear it, you can play it."

In his book *What to Listen for in Music*, Aaron Copland distinguishes between three kinds of listening—the sensuous, the expressive, and the sheerly musical. Copland says that "most listeners are not sufficiently conscious of this third plane" and suggests that "what the reader should strive for, then, is a more active kind of listening."

The severe experience which Charlotte Joko Beck had with that professor might have sent me from the room on the first day, crying "The horror! The horror!" Presently, I'm learning piano with my son Peter, who's eleven; we've been practicing together for about three years now, and Diane, our teacher, is entirely more flexible and forgiving than the professor from Oberlin. But when it comes to making a poem, to the endless revisions, the drafts, the months and years it can take, isn't the experience sometimes or often just that demanding? Don't we keep coming back, trying multiple variations, trying to get it right? When a poem isn't working, it really can be as if something or someone very rigorous is saying: "No. You haven't quite got it yet. That's not it. Keep at it. Come back tomorrow. Next week. Next month. Next year."

Many poems I see, many poems I write, are like drafts of a translation from another language: some of the information may be of real interest, there's potential there, but it hasn't been worked or played enough into its full possibility. Most poems, in my experience, turn for home too soon. I know you can also over-work something, flog a dead horse, as they say, but with most poems, I don't think we give enough time finding out what our ear wants (the phrase is from the composer John Harbison). Eliot calls this skill of listening "the auditory imagination." On some lucky occasions, the thoughts arrive as music; that certainly can and does happen. But it doesn't happen enough, at least not for me. And that is when we have to "labor to be beautiful," as Yeats says in the poem "Adam's Curse." It's very reassuring, by the way, to look at drafts and revisions of poems by fine poets, Yeats's among them, and see how long the poet was stumbling around, lost in the wrong syllables, before the piece gradually began to find its shape and sound.

Sometimes we can read a stunning poem and say to ourselves: "How did she do it? How did she sit down and just pour all that out? It's amazing. I couldn't do that—I'm just not that smart." Well, she didn't do it that way, our hypothetical poet. She wrote three lines on one day in one notebook and seven lines three months later in another notebook and four lines one day (or night) in another notebook and then, on some other day (or night) of her life, she was able to say to herself: "If I bring this together, and this, and this, I think there'll be a poem." And she does it, and there is. Shelley, in his *Defence of Poetry*, says that in poetry we detect "the before-unapprehended relations of things." And so, often, it is the ear which, weeks or months after we have poured out separate portions of language, says of them: "They want to be together." And if we can listen to that faculty within us, if we can take our time, if we can let the ear do its work (and play), we will perhaps have the makings of a poem. We may have more to do then, after the fragments are assembled, to find the final voice and the pattern the poem requires; that, too, involves the ear.

In his poem "Listening," William Stafford describes his father's acute powers of hearing, his being able to detect even "a moth in the dark against the screen." That's a good legacy, I think, the poet's father's observed behavior. It suggests the fertility of right listening. "Inviting the quiet," which the father is seen to do, suggests an openness to experience that will enable us to be touched by many things from all kinds of other places, both what is right there in front of us and also the invisible, unheard world within and around the world our senses detect.

Our culture not only does not encourage, but works against, such subtlety of listening. Do our young people feel listened to? Are they encouraged to speak out their thought? The consequences of the failure to listen to them are dreadful, and all about us. In her book *For Their Own Good*, Alice Miller writes of children who were able to express their anger (among other emotions) in childhood, learn to integrate it into their behavior, and do not need to strike out at others when they do not understand their emotions. From William Stafford's poem, we can't tell whether the listening for wild things which so inspired the children also extended to things of the mind, or the heart, or the soul, but for my purposes today, I'm taking the father's actions, like the demanding requirements of the professor of piano, as symbolic of the wisdom of listening as we could apply it to all areas of life.

I once read a review of a poetry collection by Wendell Berry in which the reviewer wrote: "The very bright and unschooled wife of a friend has said that of all the creatures here on earth, we are the only ones who don't know how to be here." That phrase has stayed with me, sometimes occurs to me as almost a negative mantra when I have screwed up some aspect of my life—*Don't know how to be here. Don't know how to be here*—almost like a self-taunting in the adult playground. One of the main ways we don't know how to be here is in our not knowing how to listen to one another and in our forgetting of what can happen to us when we really feel we are listened to. How often do we feel genuinely listened to? In how many relationships? How rare or unusual an experience is that?

Brenda Ueland, in her essay *Tell Me More*, describes her experience with a father who was not endowed with the gift of listening. He was, she tells us, "such a wonderful man, and reaching out to me and wanting to know me! But he could not. He could not listen." Elsewhere in the essay, she writes, better than anyone else I know, about "the great and powerful thing that listening is . . . a magnetic and strange thing, a creative force."

Sometimes a poet comes to a late realization of something positive which took place in childhood of which s/he was unaware at the time. Robert Hayden, in "Those Winter Sundays," comes to a profound realization about a once-maligned father. At the end of the poem, he memorably questions what he really had known "of love's austere and lonely offices." The poem is filled with references to sounds—the breaking of wood for the early morning fire, the chronic angers (most likely between the parents, most likely shouting), the indifferent communication with the father—and then, in that final, astonishing line, the poet's awareness of not-knowing. It's an extraordinary presence, that word "austere," an extraordinary exception, the only example of rising rhythm (in a single word) in the entire poem, the only iambic among all the crashing trochees, the falling rhythms, such as "blueblack" and "weekday," which dominate the poem. The piece is filled with tough consonants too, and though "austere" belongs to a chain of assonance in the poem—"ached . . . anger . . . indifferently"—still, its singular rising rhythm, invoked in the poem's final line, leaps to the ear.

Whenever I hear the anguished question of those two last lines, and the word "offices," I shiver, thinking, whenever I hear it, of the floating chanting of nuns or monks in their dark, gleaming choir stalls, the monastic offices I know well from my Catholic background. Robert, the child, the poet-to-be, must really have listened in those early years; listened, and remembered. As a boy, he would not have been articulate yet, not in possession of the vocabulary so beautifully on display in this well-loved poem; but some intuitive intelligence in him stored those sounds and those images, and one day, much later in his life, he was able to bring all this together and come to the poem's healing conclusion. It achieves a depth of statement he could never have previewed, one he could hardly have felt himself capable of making when he first began to summon those disparate materials onto the page. I don't know how many drafts the poem went through, but I have no doubt that it was a listening to the materials of the poem itself, the words in their sequences of sound, which strongly contributed to the conclusion he finally came to.

I'm aware that in these remarks I am short-changing the image, something I'm not usually inclined to do: poems live also by their images—we know that. But today I'm choosing to stress sound. Mark Twain, who famously says, "Wagner's music is better than it sounds," also says that only an inferior writer—he cites Cooper—settles for the "approximate word." "When a person has a poor ear for words," says Twain, "the result is a literary flatting and sharping; you perceive what he is intending to say, but you also perceive that he doesn't say it." The difference between the approximate word and the right word, the word you really want, Twain tells us, is the difference between the lightning bug and the lightning.

I like what Auden says, that "in poetry, words are not the handmaiden of thought; words are the mother of thought." So it's not that we find a "neat idea" for which we then find words; rather, it's the words themselves, the erupting and flowing of a few clusters of syllables, which alert us to implications that we explore into and through the poem. We are listening into the language. This is a complex issue, the genesis of a poem, and there surely are poems whose initial impulse is at least equally visual and/ or dramatic, but I believe that if the poem is to unfold to its true potential, to become a real, memorable "sonic structure," then the words themselves must play a significant part in the development of whatever argument or narrative the poem comes up with. We need to draw on all the resources of the language if we are to encompass the experience or awareness which asks a poem of us.

Poems proceed and live by contrast. In Judith Hemschemeyer's poem "The Dirty-Billed Freeze Footy," which I first read in *Tangled Vines*, a collection of mother and daughter poems edited by Lyn Lifshin, there are fifteen lines, fourteen of them in free verse couplets, and all of them directly observant of an eccentric mother. In the middle of the poem we encounter: "and you had done it: / reduced our queen to warm and helpless rubble." In the Hayden poem, it was the word "austere" that was the only one of its kind, the only rising rhythm; in this poem, there is only one metaphor, only one elegantly cadenced iambic pentameter, and the two combine in a single line which stands on its own, among couplets, in the center—"reduced our queen to warm and helpless rubble." How we feel its differentness and its presence! Poems live by just this kind of variety, these kinds of shifts. Suppose we were to be driving across a flat landscape all day, all day, and suddenly we glimpsed a high hill, the only thing like it in the entire landscape:

how grateful we would be! Such relief in the map of our long day—vertical relief.

These are the kinds of dynamics, shifts, which keep a poem alive. Music has its dynamic markings—crescendo, mezzo-forte, andante, allegro, and the like—and it deploys its effects variously. Poetry, too, relies on contrast—the play between the monosyllabic and the polysyllabic, between Anglo-Saxon directness and Latinate elaboration, between plain statement and figurative, between high diction and low diction, long rhythms counterpointed by shorter, and so on. Poems live by these mixtures. In the case of Judith Hemschemeyer's poem, the poet's ear helped her to that decision to locate the only metaphor, and the only traditional cadence, in solitude in the center of the poem. Her ear served her well.

Next to that poem in the anthology, there's another poem by Judith Hemschemeyer, "The Survivors" in which the mother is seen this time as a tragically insecure and possessive figure; the poems ends: "We are her angels / Burned so crisp / We crumble when we try to touch." Same poet, same mother. Different occasion, very different response. As we listen and attend to each individual occasion, the better chance we have of finding the words, images, rhythms expressive of its particularity. The alternative—the lack of attentive listening, the use of colorless language—can result in kind of dullness we're all familiar with in both our writing and our reading lives.

There are many more matters to do with listening which I haven't time to go into today, but I want to mention two of them in passing. One is how animal-like we become when we listen: we revert, become creaturely, alert, aware in a newly heightened way of being in the body. In his outstandingly ingenious essay *Goatfoot Milktongue Twinbird*, Donald Hall states that Mother Goose is a better poet than W. H. Auden. He's right, of course. It has to do with the rhythm, with the way the rhythms *get to us*, to our bodily selves. In her book *Centering*, M.C. Richards, a poet as well as potter, writes: "With listening. . . . It is the total person who hears. Sometimes the skin seems to be the best listener, as it prickles and thrills, say to a sound or a silence." And A. E. Housman, in his lecture "The Name and Nature of Poetry," tells how he tries to keep lines of poetry from straying into his mind when he is shaving in the morning. If some lines of poetry do come to him, he writes, the skin bristles and the razor "ceases to act." And Emily Dickinson, in a letter, famously describes feeling so cold that no fire can warm her in the presence of poetry, feeling as if the top of her head is being taken off.

I am also intrigued by who we can sometimes become, in poetry, by means of our own inner listening, the renewal of the sense of self that becomes possible if we can manage the attentiveness each occasion requires of us. In poems, Richard Hugo tells us, there is an initial subject and a generated subject. That generated subject, that second subject, as a composer might say, is often just that, a person who arises within us, an identity with dimensions, perspectives and powers we did not suspect at the beginning of the poem. In the last of his "Six Winter Privacy Poems," which is called "Listening to Bach," Robert Bly writes: "I am alone, yet someone else is with me," and that is what I would call a generated presence. In many situations, there's the sense of an identity that lies in a darkness not lit by human naming, a self not always available to our awareness but which can, on occasion—the occasion of deep music, for example, or of exceptional introspection—make itself known to us. I am interested in that Self who can appear within the self, the one we can sometimes generate in poems by means of an inner listening. "Yet someone else is with me."

By countless acts of attentiveness, we incorporate into ourselves, and articulate, a deeper being, one through whom a healing becomes possible. By such transformations we can begin to hold ourselves to a different standard of conduct in the world. I don't mean that we become less human but rather more human, more fully human: we round out the sense of who we are and what might be the powers of the language we have been given to use. A poem is one way of coming to know our true dimensions. We generate that coming to know through the most intense yet relaxed attentiveness to the inner rings of being and to the new sounds that we become capable of making with the usually familiar words. A poem is a chance to "heal reality with reality," as Yehuda Amichai once said, and to be more fully aware of the potential of each lived moment. The goal is to be human, with all the freedoms and responsibilities which that state entails.

The wiser self is not always subsumed into the poet. Sometimes it is expressed as a separate identity in dramatic terms—an other—though we often sense the poet is dramatizing an aspect of the self. Among the poems I particularly admire which do that are "The Flower of Air" by Gabriela Mistral; "Guardian Angel" by Rolf Jacobsen; "I am not I" by Juan Ramón Jiménez; "The Delight Song of Tsaio-Talee" by N. Scott Momaday; "Ego-Tripping" by Nikki Giovanni; "The Fish" by Elizabeth Bishop; "Filling Station" by Elizabeth Bishop; "The Man Watching" by Rainer Maria Rilke; "Requiem" by Anna Akhmatova; "Summer Solstice New York City" by Sharon Olds; "Prayer During a Time My Son is Having Seizures" by Sharon Olds; "Journey to the Interior" by Theodore Roethke; "Julia" by Wendy Rose; and "Prayer for Marilyn Monroe" by Ernesto Cardenal.

Rilke writes somewhere—in a letter, as I remember—that the poet is like one who stands on the deck of a ship being rowed across the ocean and strikes up a song when the rowing has become ragged, the one who provides a melody and rhythm which help the rowers pick up their pace and resume working more closely with one another to move the vessel forward. We need to be listening, to have an ear for the faltering of the rhythm and then to provide song. Those oars, those rowers, are also inside us, and sometimes, just sometimes, we can generate our own music and regain the momentum we had thought was lost. If we do it right, it will cross into other lives and contribute to their reality.

A poem is always, in some proportion, about its own sound. The poet's ear works to restore the magical, physical properties of words. The poem wants to cast a spell, even a casual one, but a spell, nevertheless. A lot of contemporary poetry is strong visually, and presents situations to us in striking dramatic, visual, dreamlike ways—and that is one of its strengths. But without its particular patterns of sounds, the poem would not be creating its effect. It's easy to forget this. I can forget it myself.

Whitman says: "I think I will do nothing for a long time but listen, / And accrue what I hear into myself—and let sounds contribute toward me." This has been, pretty much, my theme this morning, how listening to sounds contributes to our poems and to the lives we lead with and among one another. Let Linda Hogan have the last words:

Blessed
are those who listen
when no one is left to speak.

Annual meeting of the National Association
of Poetry Therapy, Minneapolis, May 1994.

Failure

In 1992, a fourth collection of my poems was published. I worked hard on that book; one poem in particular, about my mother, took me more than three years to finish. I think I managed to get into that poem a good deal of the intense confusion and grief I felt in the months following her death, and it is likely one of the best things I have written. The poem is a failure. There are two or three other poems in the collection of which I might say, as I say of the poem about my mother: "I can't do that very often." At the same time, the book that contains these poems is a failure.

Why should I say that? I am hardly sorry for myself. Nor am I boasting of failure. I remember a teacher in France, long ago, Bernard Ehret, who used to come into the staff room at the Lycée de Garçons in Chambéry and declare, with a broad smile on his face: "Je suis modeste et je ne le cache pas!" (I am modest and I do not hide the fact.) Failure is something I expect and accept as a writer, and today I want to try to say what I mean by calling one of my better poems, and my new book, a failure. Along the way, I'll pass on the thoughts of some other writers that I have found helpful on this subject.

I am borrowing, of course, from George Orwell. In his essay "Why I Write," Orwell says that by the time you have perfected a style of writing, you have outgrown it. "I have not written a novel for seven years," he writes, "but I hope to write another fairly soon. It is bound to be a failure, every book is a failure, but I know with some clarity what kind of book I want to write." I like how Orwell tosses that phrase onto on the page between a couple of commas— "every book is a failure"—for him it's a given—and moves right on to the next thought.

Let's look at his statement for a moment. Most of us wouldn't think of *Animal Farm*, for example, as a failure—I certainly don't. But if it is, at least to some extent, might it have been the "full consciousness" of intent he also speaks of that is part of the problem? Might the whole thing have been too willed, too clearly illustrative of a prior concept, rather than sufficiently imagined along the way? And, in general terms, might every book have to seem a failure to the writer so that the next one becomes necessary? Is there a way in which we can see acknowledgment of a book's "failure" not as something that quenches the imagination, that robs the writer of confidence for future work, but rather as an incentive to—forgive the hearty phrases—do it better, to get it right, next time?

The "it" is constantly changing, of course, which is part of the problem, part of the challenge. Orwell says that a style reaches perfection always too late, which may mean that some new content has begun to suggest itself for which a fresh style is needed ("Form is never more than an extension of content," in Robert Creeley's formulation). For a poet, it can also be that a new way of using language, some rhythmical surge of phrases or pulsing of unprecedented syntax, is proposing itself independent of any foreseeable content. In either case, while you are still coming into full articulation of the original subject, as the "full consciousness" is earnestly at work on the topic at hand, the good old anarchic unconscious is whispering of new horizons and subverting the whole enterprise. Eliot describes every attempt as

> . . . a wholly new start, and a different kind of failure
> Because one has only learnt to get the better of words
> For the thing one no longer has to say, or the way in
>   which
> One is no longer disposed to say it.

As new subjects occur to us, or are thrust upon us, we need real flexibility of response if we are to catch them with the palpable forms of poems. How do we stay faithful to what we had thought we wanted to write about while letting in freshly generated ideas, or forms, which may or may not be the true subject, not be organic to that subject matter? Such tension of decisions is always with the writer, and a certain formal restlessness, characteristic of many great artists, seems appropriate through the course of a lifetime.

A single lifetime isn't long enough, very obviously, to act on everything that is proposed internally by our own imaginations, and a feeling of failure may consist not only in the suspicion that style and content have somehow fallen out in a particular work and begun to renege on their original vows, but also in a feeling of incompletion. Just as we finally abandon each work rather than complete it (to quote Valéry), so, too, we run out of time to carry out all the tasks we can envision. "I'll go to my grave with a million things unsaid," I remarked once to a student, meaning to sound matter-of-fact rather than grandiosely mournful, and probably failing at that. (This was the same student who had written, in an end-of-term assessment: "I'm worried about what I'm avoiding in my work," and the topic of avoidance, its intimate links to failure, is a whole talk, or two, in itself.) But while it's impossible not to refer to the griefs that can be associated with failure, my main purpose here is to rescue the word from merely dire connotations, dust it off a little, and then return it to its place in the life of the writer.

I don't see the sense of incompletion as something necessarily desperate, but rather as an inevitable element, one I need to learn to accept and even embrace: as artists, we have to acknowledge the approximateness of what we can accomplish. This awareness is not going to stop me from taking on large projects, from robing myself in some ancient naiveté as I sit down to take on something all the sensible parts of me know (and shriek at me) I can never manage. Foreknowledge of failure is not a lid on our aspiration. In an interview, Eavan Boland, a contemporary Irish poet, talks about working at a rock face, and finding in it, just occasionally, "a bit of silver, a bit of base metal." She goes on to say that the failure rate must exceed the success rate, that "all poets need to have a sane and normalized relationship with their failure rate."

Such remarks, in their matter-of-factness, seem to me to be exactly helpful. Here's a working writer, a first-rate one, who sees acquaintance with her own failure as a very necessary part of her own process. Once again, it's not a matter of self-pity: simply, we need to stay in dialogue with whoever inside us is able to be ruthless about the second-rate work we frequently do, and is never afraid to name it, someone who can "kill the darlings" (Faulkner's phrase) every time it becomes necessary (and that will be often). We need to see the words "success" and "failure," such hardened polarities, as a large part of the problem, and get ourselves out from under the shadow of such dualities. And the separating of what's good from what's not, in revision after revision, should perhaps be reinstated as an intuitive, muscular activity rather than as a primarily cerebral one, something carried out, as Boland has it, by a worker at a rock face or, to improvise a figure of my own, like a bouncer in a bar. Throw the rascals out!

Here's another quotation, one that I read in a biography of Einstein, where, once again, an inner process is imaged as a physical activity. Toward the end of his life, Sir Isaac Newton wrote this:

> I do not know what I may appear to the world; but
> to myself I seem to have been only like a boy, playing
> on the sea-shore, and diverting myself, in now and
> then finding a smoother pebble or prettier shell
> than ordinary, whilst the great ocean of truth lay all
> undiscovered before me.

While there's something rueful about this admission, I suspect that even if Newton had guessed early on in his inventive life that it would come down to this, he would not been likely to have "ceased from exploring."

Should we allow our sense of our own limitations to shrink us into a sense of inferiority, and so hold back our curiosity? What can we do to answer the inner voice, the one never tiring of telling us that we won't make it but that others will, that whispers to us that our own pretensions are laughable? One thing we might do is to imagine alternative mental states, conjure landscapes where creation typically takes place. Patients suffering from certain types of cancer can be taught to do this, sometimes with startling results. One especially helpful image comes from the Spanish writer José

Ortega y Gasset.

> So many things fail to interest us, simply because they
> don't find in us enough surfaces on which to live, and
> what we have to do then is increase the number of
> planes in our mind so that a much larger number of
> themes can find a place in it at the same time.

I'll give you my own simple visualization of Ortega's state-
ment. Imagine a flock of several hundred birds looking, toward
the end of day, for a place to spend the night. They fly past the
tree that has only a branch or two and a mere couple of dozen
twigs—not enough room for them, not nearly enough surfaces.
When they detect a tree that has many branches, multiple twigs,
that's where they land and settle in. In my own experience, there
are plenty of poems I have failed to write, or to complete, because
I wasn't able to provide enough surfaces for landing, and so some
potentially powerful visions went on by. An image is, says Pound, a
"visual chord," is "that which presents an intellectual and emotional
complex in an instant of time," and the imagination needs to be
constantly renewing itself, putting forth new areas, landing sites, if
it is to receive the new subjects and new language that constantly
propose themselves to us. I feel challenged by this image, try to
keep it in mind and draw upon it rather than sink into a stupor of
imageless despair. As I get older, I find myself more excited than
ever by the issues I might be able to write about, and, at the same
time, properly humbled by my abilities to make poetry of them. I
need to work at staying open, becoming even more open, just as
I need to keep my body flexible, keep the spine supple as it ages.
The work of providing those internal surfaces also requires a tough-
ness, requires that we be prepared to shed old patterns, tired habits,
so that we can stay alert for the arrival (at any time) of possibly
astonishing words and ideas.

The very idea of success, which Eavan Boland mentioned, can
be poisoning. What is success for a poet? Not so long ago, I read an
interview with a well-known poet in which he said that a certain

critic had called him one of the five or six "best" poets writing in America today. He seemed to be approving of this statement. I have also heard a visiting poet, a fine writer and teacher, say in front of my students that another certain critic called him the "best" poet writing in America today; he passed off the remark, but why did he bring it up? Against such notions I would set the melancholy resonance of Leonardo's "Dimmi se mai fu fatto qualche cosa?" (Tell me if anything was ever done?), said as he was pouring water over a skull he planned to draw, or Eliot's reply to a friend who asked him, as they were crossing a London street one day: "Tom, do you know you're good?" "No," said Eliot, "do you?"

I would also set against them these words of Virginia Woolf, talking of Shakespeare's imagined sister, she who died without having written a word:

> I am talking of the common life which is the real life and not of the little separate lives which we live as individuals . . . if we have the habit of freedom and the courage to write exactly what we think; if we escape a little from the common sitting-room and see human beings not always in their relation to each other but in relation to reality . . . then the opportunity will come and the dead poet who was Shakespeare's sister will put on the body which she has so often laid down . . . I maintain that she would come if we worked for her, and that so to work, even in poverty and obscurity, is worthwhile.

Here again is the idea of work, the rock face, the persistent exploring—the "real work," as Gary Snyder calls it. The vanity of the idea of success, and the corresponding polarity of failure, too often sets us, fellow artists, fellow human beings, against one another; the result is that we expend our energies in senseless competitiveness, thinking ourselves failures as we see others winning awards, prizes, critical acknowledgment. While I myself am hardly immune to these kinds of envies and depressions, what I try to do is to let them rise up, in all their unreality, have their vain say, and then let them go; I try to clear myself, get myself back to the reality of the work I have to do, which involves reality itself. That is where my obligation lies; that is where I am aimed.

The title of the book I am working on now, *In The Carpenter's House*, came to me one day as I was sweeping the floor of a small building in northern Minnesota. It stands a few yards from the main cabin on our land and it's a beautifully built structure: post and beam, wooden dowels, oak beams, pine paneling—and the floor is plywood. Still plywood, six years after the building went up. This is the "studio" where I do my work when we are in the woods, where friends stay when they come to visit. What will it take to put the floor in, the final floor of fir or oak? More money than I can presently come up with. A composer friend of mine, John Foley, stayed in the studio some years ago, just after it went up, while we were working on a piece together; and long after that experience, as I was sweeping the floor one time, I was saying to him, in my mind: "See, John, the floor is still plywood, just as it was when you were first up here five years ago. It still isn't finished." And suddenly this provisional floor seemed to me emblematic of so much in my own writing and in my own life: it might never be finished, never be "final."

The carpenter's own house is often, even notoriously, in that kind of shape while the carpenter works at completing the homes of other people. And I found this image not only liberating about a number of things in my life but also, instantly, a strong contender as the subject of a cycle of poems I would write that would then be set to music by John! I have been working at this cycle for some time now, inflamed with a sense of its possibilities, but I have a long way to go. I may get it done, and again, I may not. "Ars longa, vita brevis," says Hippocrates. "The lyf so short, the craft so long to lerne," says Chaucer. "And so it goes," says a certain contemporary writer of fiction.

You can expect too little from your own work in its relation to how you live your life. You can also dangerously expect it to substitute for the ongoing work of maintaining real relationships:

an account of the toll that an excessive focus on writing can take on the quality of your living would have to be a long chapter in a book about writers and failure. You can expect too much of your writing, and, once again, there's a tension of decisions here that the writer must live with.

Let me tell you a story, both for and against a remark by D. H. Lawrence that I've always found helpful: "One sheds one's sickness in books." This suggests the therapeutic function of writing— that you can heal yourself, as an artist, by becoming conscious of something that would otherwise fester in the unconscious, stirring up all kinds of unclearly motivated and bizarre behavior. I think there's a great deal of truth in this; it is not the whole story, however, and I'll show you what I mean with an illustration from my own psychological life.

In 1976, I finished a long poem called "Sun Exercises," an extended elegy for my father Eddie, who died suddenly in 1960, when I was nineteen. It was an elaborate piece that combined some direct and heartfelt mourning with, as I see it now, some pretty indigestible references to both hatha yoga and Egyptian mythology. Like the elegy for my mother in my most recent book, it, too, is a failure—though on a rather grander scale, perhaps! But at the time, I was rather pleased with the poem, and when it was published as a book, in a beautiful small edition by a local press, with striking illustrations by Annie Hayes, I felt quite good indeed about it. A month or two after its publication, and after I had given a number of readings in which I read the poem in its entirety (it took about half an hour), I had a dream in which my father was dying in a small motel somewhere up on the north shore of Lake Superior: he began to vomit, and out of his mouth came long rolls of white material on which there were many small, dark markings. It went on and on for hours, this flowing vomiting. The dream made a very strong impression on me and brought with it a huge affect of sadness that I did not quite understand.

A few days later, I realized that what my father had been vomiting up in the dream was the long, recently published poem in which I imagined I had shed the sickness of sixteen years of mourning for him, shed it with a certain amount of public and "po biz" attention, leading myself to believe that the grief at his death, so long subverting my joy, was past, and I could get on with my life. My interpretation—and it remains only that—was that the dream was compensating for a considerable smugness (and relief) in my conscious thinking; it was reminding me that though one can "shed one's sickness in books," the matter is never quite as simple as that, and that even after sixteen years of a certain kind of mourning, I could not bring it to closure with such apparent finality. It was showing me that the grieving would never be done. The corrective effect of the nightmarish dream image has stayed with me and continues to teach me that I have no choice but to stay in dialogue with a number of obsessions, of which the death of the father is one. "Failure" comes in thinking that the poem has settled the topic once and for all, or in the expectation that the topic itself will ever be quite done with.

In his poem "For Sheridan," Robert Lowell writes that as we get older, we learn "that what I intended and failed could never have happened—and must be done better."

In other words—and it's a beautifully expressed paradox— what we have in mind to do early on as poets is both misguided and essential. What we think we need to tackle is always different from our early notions of it—we will fail if we attempt to flesh out the synopsis in extreme detail—and yet our instincts are, in general, accurate. If a poem itself is "best when generally not perfectly understood, " as Coleridge says, then perhaps we need to bring a similar latitude of expectation to our own writing lives and learn to be less rigid, relax the parameters of both what the task seems to us to be and what our ambitions for ourselves ("the idea of success") asks of us. Might that help us to do things "better"? One way to proceed is to become more philosophical, precisely as Lowell is being, and to live with the tensions of the paradox as he states it in the poem. If we can come to the realization that, as Tadeusz Rozewicz says of his poetry, "it has many tasks / to which it will never do justice," then we might possibly go about the work of poetry less dependent on recognition of our worth from external sources, more aware of ourselves as permanently apprenticed to the exploration of consciousness, to what another contemporary Polish poet, Czeslaw Milosz, calls "the passionate pursuit of reality."

Part of the problem, then, is seeing failure itself as a problem that drags us down rather than as a "losing of the scent" (one of the original meanings of the word), with the suggestion that pursuit can, with patience and with persistence, be resumed. In his book *Care of the Soul*, Thomas Moore, a psychotherapist, sees failure as "a source of potential soul," sees failing at something as usefully antidotal to overly high expectations. When ambition and ideas of perfection are tempered by failure, he says, something is incarnated in us that is specifically human, whereas "perfection belongs to an imaginary world." He goes on to say: "Failure is a mystery, not a problem," that we should learn to "incorporate failure into our work so that it doesn't literally devastate us." Boris Pasternak, in a memoir, writes that "in life it is more necessary to lose than to gain. A seed will only germinate if it dies." Such remarks, which obviously have spiritual as well as purely literary implications, hearten me, and neither is far in essence from those of George Orwell or Eavan Boland or Isaac Newton or Virginia Woolf or Jose Ortega y Gasset. There's a consensus that the job is far larger than the worker: we are committed to trying to bring to life something whose measure not one of us can take in, even in a long lifetime. This should not stop us.

For all its possibly wild internal energy, however, the enterprise needs to be grounded in the revelation of what lies all about us in physical terms. When Emily Dickinson says "Nature is a Haunted House—but Art—A House that tries to be haunted," she brilliantly suggests not only the tantalizing polarities of the world we live in but also the necessity of our artistic commitment to it if our expressiveness is be faithful to the human experience we have been undergoing since our first breaths.

I'll take one last example out of my own life. When our first child was born eight years ago—a son, Peter—I was so wonder-struck by the event, and by the early months of his life, that I found myself ashamed of language itself: it seemed such a crude system of signs, such a weak vehicle, to convey the complex of emotions I was going through. In the second half of a poem I wrote at this time, "To Show Peter the World," I talk first about this sense of the inadequacy of language and then come to a realization about what I must do:

> There are days, child, I have woken
> ashamed of the names, wanting
> for your entering, fresher ones
> for what you will come to know,
> and what I must learn to do, all
> over again, is trust the necessity,
> the endlessness, the grace of our naming,
> which is human, which is what we do,
> and sound again around lips and teeth and tongue,
> and roll again down bones and veins
> familiar syllables, yes, the usual ones,
> until they assume the unknown again,
> until no name's familiar, and learn
>
> not only to wander with you
> the present borders of our naming
> but to be there to watch and listen
> as you begin going on beyond,
> making your names for the things, as
> Peter shown Peter the world, this place
> into which we have only brought you,
> and in which we must leave you.

I haven't talked about many of the darkest aspects of failure, which are very real, and can lead to a paralysis—"the apple unbitten in the palm," as Philip Larkin has called it—which is living death for the writer. In certain kinds of failures, we can almost feel the cells crumbling, and these little deaths can accumulate until the whole system is poisoned. What I have wanted to get across, however, is that we need to learn to live with failure and, in a sense, to die to the idea of it by incorporating it, even embracing it—I think of the image "our sister the death of the body" of Francis of Assisi. If we are aimed toward reality, if we are apprenticed to depicting it, naturally we will "fail," daily. But we can do better than live in the shadow of such dualities as success and failure.

The most useful work each one of us can do, as writers at any level of experience, is to become a "bigger container," in Charlotte Joko Beck's term, of whatever reality is, more ready to make use of what comes into us, in all its bewildering possibilities, so that we can be those on whom, to quote Henry James's wonderfully unreasonable formulation, "nothing is lost." It is an old idea that the end is the journey itself, and that in the experiencing and accepting and embracing of failure, we become most fully human. Through daily personal and artistic discipline we can work to be more receptive, even if we often come to realize that the maps we have made are not the territory, that our persistent examining leads us to the conviction that, as Auden says, the truth is a silence toward which words can only point. We can see this as a pathology, a problem, or as a mystery, one to live as authentically as possible.

In a short piece called *Some Notes on Struggle and Joy*, Olga Broumas, a Greek-American poet, says that she imagines the infinite "because it gives my soul pleasure, because imagining the infinite is the vocation of the soul." It is another old idea that the body-bound soul has forgotten its limitless capacities, and that the kinds of joy it is equipped for are not those the world is usually inclined to give. You cannot expect to get back from the world any external reward ("success") commensurate with the devotion, craft, time, soul you have put into your work; the joy lies, finally, elsewhere. All we can do is, as Yeats recommends in "To A Friend Whose Work Has Come to Nothing," is exult in secret—which is, he says, "of all things known . . . the most difficult."

Talk to the Split Rock Arts Program, July 1992.

Poetry and Walking

My interest in the connection between poetry and walking began in a British high school over forty years ago with William Wordsworth: my teachers read him to us with great relish, and the subject has become of interest to me as a poet in ways I could never have anticipated back then. I remain grateful for my first contact with Wordsworth in general—with the *Lyrical Ballads*, "The Prelude," the "Immortality Ode," with "Lines Composed a Few Miles Above Tintern Abbey." On a family vacation in the Wye Valley, a dozen years ago, my brother Peter and I went walking the river path at dawn, upstream from the Abbey. We saw swans drifting under pale skeins of mist and, on the opposite bank of the river, two young horses thundering up and down, up and down, out of the sheer joy of running, as it seemed to us.

Walking played a large part both in Wordsworth's life and in his compositional process: he relied on it, as I in my own way have come to do. According to his sister Dorothy, William walked out "every morning, generally alone, and brings in a large treat almost every time he goes out." By "treat" she means, of course, lines of poetry. Thomas De Quincey estimated that Wordsworth, by the time he was sixty-five, had walked close to 180,000 miles! And in Thoreau's essay on walking, one finds this anecdote: a traveler, arriving at the house while Wordsworth was out, asked the poet's servant to show him her master's study, and received this reply: "Here is his library, but his study is out of doors."

Another major influence on me was A. E. Housman, author of the impeccably melancholy *A Shropshire Lad*. "Loveliest of Trees," a particularly well-loved poem, ends with the poet's resolve to go about the woodlands and "see the cherry hung with snow," and the "going" is, of course, on foot. But it is a piece of prose by Housman, a section of his famous lecture "The Name and Nature of Poetry," which has been especially helpful to me in thinking about the relationship between poetry and walking.

In this clear, quirky piece, Housman, arguably the greatest classical scholar of his time in England, describes poetry as "more physical than intellectual" and says that he tries not to think of poetry while shaving because if he does, his skin bristles and the razor "ceases to act." He then gives this accounting of his poetic process, and while I am mindful of D. H. Lawrence's admonition to "trust the tale, not the teller," I have always found this little telling of Housman's convincing:

> Having drunk a pint of beer at luncheon—beer is
> a sedative to the brain, and my afternoons are the
> least intellectual portion of my life—I would go out
> for a walk of two or three hours. As I went along,
> thinking of nothing in particular, only looking at
> things around me and following the progress of
> the seasons, there would flow into my mind, with
> sudden and unaccountable emotion, sometimes a
> line or two of verse, sometimes a whole stanza at
> once, accompanied, not preceded, by a vague notion
> of the poem which they were destined to form part
> of. Then there would usually be a lull of an hour or
> so, then perhaps the spring would bubble up again.
> I say bubble up, because, so far as I could make out,
> the source of the suggestions thus proffered to the
> brain was an abyss which I have already had occasion
> to mention, the pit of the stomach. When I got home
> I wrote them down, leaving gaps, and hoping that
> further inspiration might be forthcoming another day.
> Sometimes it was, if I took my walks in a receptive
> and expectant frame of mind; but sometimes the
> poem had to be taken in hand and completed by the
> brain, which was apt to be a matter of trouble and
> anxiety, involving trial and disappointment, and
> sometimes ending in failure. I happen to remember
> distinctly the genesis of the piece which stands last
> in my first volume. Two of the stanzas, I do not say
> which, came into my head, just as they are printed,
> while I was crossing the corner of Hampstead Heath

between Spaniard's Inn and the footpath to Temple Fortune. A third stanza came with a little coaxing after tea. One more was needed, but it did not come: I had to turn to and compose it myself, and that was a laborious business. I wrote it thirteen times, and it was more than a twelvemonth before I got it right.

Many elements of this rich paragraph are worth exploring, but I will confine myself to two of them—firstly, the "looking at things around me and following the progress of the seasons" and, secondly, "there would flow into my mind, with sudden and unaccountable emotion, sometimes a line or two of verse, sometimes a whole stanza at once"—which I believe have something to do with the rhythms aroused by walking.

For Housman, the looking, the thinking of nothing in particular, precedes the appearance of the lines of poetry. When he is able to pay attention to the immediate surroundings, when the anxiety engendered by leaping about between thoughts of past and present and future is gone—or has, at the least, subsided—when he is able to be present, mindful, then there is more room than usual within his relatively emptied consciousness for all the visual (and other sensory) particulars that present themselves to the walker.

Mary Oliver, a contemporary American poet, has some thoughts on this subject in her poem "Yes! No!," where she writes of walking "not in haste but slowly, looking at everything and calling out / Yes! No!" In an interview, she says:

> I take walks. Walks work for me. I enter some arena that is neither conscious nor unconscious. It's a joke here in town: I take a walk and I'm found standing still somewhere. This is not a walk to arrive; this is a walk that's part of a process.

Earlier in the century, Eleanor Farjeon describes walking with Edward Thomas, an English poet known for his influence on, and walks with, Robert Frost:

To walk with Edward Thomas in any countryside
was to see, hear, smell and know it with fresh senses.
He was as alert to what was happening in and on the
earth and the air above it as an animal in the grass
or a bird on a tree. Just as certain friends who share
their thoughts with you will sharpen your thinking,
he had the effect, when you took the road together, of
quickening your seeing and hearing through his own
keen eyes and ears. You would not walk that road
again as you did before. You would know it in a new
way.

Farjeon tells of a walk in Sussex with Edward Thomas and D.
H. Lawrence, himself one of the great poets of the century:

At that time I walked with the long lope that matched
Edward's negligent stride. He covered ground fast
without any appearance of hurry. It was too fast for
Lawrence, who soon said, "I must teach you to walk
like a tramp. When you are going to walk all day you
must learn to amble and rest every mile or so". . . .
Lawrence was in his angelic, child-like mood. . . . Our
talk that day seldom touched on the things that irked
him unendurably. In one of the deep bottoms, where
the whitebeams looked like trees in silver blossom,
he cried, "We must be springlike!" and broke green
branches and stuck them round our hats.

I like to think of the often testy Bert Lawrence in an "angelic,
child-like mood." How much credit for that, I wonder, can one
assign to the company, how much to the walking, how much to
the whitebeams?

All around, as one walks, are the inscapes and instresses, as
Gerard Manley Hopkins calls them, of the natural or the urban
world (to make what I know is a crude distinction). For my own
part, if I can be not crammed with thinking, and set out in the kind
of "receptive and expectant frame of mind" that Housman speaks
of, and if walking can contribute to the further emptying out of

the kind of mental chatter with which we constantly interpret the world to ourselves, then, in the unhierarchical nature of things observed, anything at all can make an impression, can initiate an image, a rhythm, a phrase; can propose a theme, a pattern. You do not look over-consciously for these things—looking being a good in itself—but rather let the things around you become endlessly suggestive to the imagination.

I often think of John Keats's sentence, from a letter: "And if a sparrow come before my window, I take part in its existence and peck about at the gravel." If one substitutes "eyes" for "window," then here is a fair example of what can happen when you are on foot, moving along the ground, well-grounded in a motioned way. Your response is by no means always empathetic; sometimes the revelation is simply of the complete otherness of things, and in this regard Lawrence's "I didn't know him" often occurs to me, though this was said of a big pike, and from a small boat, not on foot, on land. "He was born in front of my sunrise," Lawrence goes on. "And I, a many-fingered horror of daylight to him, have made him die."

It is very real, walking, real time over real ground, and with everything around *being* honest in what it is—everything just, after all, merely and miraculously being—a sparrow, an oak, a daffodil, a wheelbarrow—this is no place or time for dissembling. Nor is it a place or time for favoring the human over the nonhuman: walking, I experience myself not as owner or appropriator of what I am seeing, but as merely one more example of consciousness in the landscape. The things I am among and pass by—the species, the tribes, the varieties, the variations—remind me continually of the extraordinary fertility and otherness of the contents of the natural and the humanly created worlds. And as a walker, I am one such thing—only, in this case, a walking thing. Looking, like the walking that induces and enhances it, is a great leveler.

A poem is a sequence of imaginative decisions, and what the walker-writer receives is, in its essence, sequential. The looking in no way ties me to a consistent, literal, linked descriptiveness or to any particular kind of poem or writing. But just as it helps to have a good hard surface if you have a mind to bounce something, sometimes the kind of relaxed observing that takes place during a walk can generate associations that take the imagination far from the literal point of departure. This interaction can also generate a greater imaginative intimacy between the observed and the invented (again, crude distinctions). I like what Francis Ponge says of the tension within images: "An image should depart from its object to show how the mind has kindled it, but it should also resemble it." Pablo Neruda's elemental odes might be one example of the kind of intimacy that can be achieved between—that radiates from—the two modes of seeing.

According to Anne Wallace, author of a recent book on walking and nineteenth-century poetry, particularly the poetry of Wordsworth, there seem to be no real histories of walking—it has been thought to be too ordinary an activity, and its immense popularity is relatively recent. There is also a frequent tendency, Wallace says, to "fall up," to neglect the process itself by dephysicalizing walking into analogy (life-as-journey). But now the books on walking and literature begin to appear. Wallace, in one of the first of them, makes an ingenious analogy; she sees Wordsworth's walking and his walking poetry as

> an extension of the Virgilian georgic accomplished by
> placing the walker in the ideological space vacated
> by the farmer. The result, which I call "peripatetic,"
> represents excursive walking as a cultivating labor
> capable of renovating both the individual and his
> society by recollecting and expressing past value.

This is from a chapter called "Walking Where the Sower Dwelt." Earlier in the book, Wallace quotes some of the many claims made for the *general* worth of walking, among them Patricia Edwards Bleyle's notion of walking as a kind of "cure," with its "sustained and regular rhythm of solitary movement through the countryside," and John Elder's notion that "the landscape and the imagination may be united through the process of walking," whereby "walking becomes an emblem of wholeness, comprehending both the person's conscious steps and pauses and the path beneath his rising and falling feet."

The phrase "rising and falling feet" inevitably makes me think of iambs and trochees, and of Oliver Wendell Holmes's description of walking as "a perpetual falling with a perpetual self-recovery" (trochees first for him), and it brings me to the large topic of the effect of walking rhythms upon the poet and its possible generating of the "sudden and unaccountable emotion" of which Housman speaks. The walking itself is, to put it plainly, pedestrian-syllabic, isochronous (equal time: left right, left right). Your stride has, in its mechanical way, no metrical mercy: it lays down a very basic rhythm track—as in, for example, the striding of marching Marines. This is quite different from the traditional poetic feet that we have inherited in English from quantitative classical prosody and modified into accentual-syllabic, to say nothing of the cadences of free verse. Classical quantitative verse is governed by the length of the syllables, and if you walked according to those ancient measures, you would be doing the fox trot, or something like it: slow, slow, quick, quick, slow. There's nothing to stop anyone from doing that (best to pick a quiet road, perhaps), but I am suggesting that the lowest of the layers of rhythms I experience when walking, that of the feet themselves, is, in its regularity, at best an indirect, if powerful, influence on the writing it provokes and enhances. Walking itself is metronomic—and we compose, as Ezra Pound says, by the cadence of the musical phrase, not the metronomic.

In languages other than English, it is possible that the consequences of the walking rhythm may be very different and somewhat more direct. When Osip Mandelstam writes of Dante that

> both the *Inferno* and, in particular, the *Purgatorio*
> glorify the human gait, the measure and rhythm of
> walking, the footstep and its form. The step, linked
> with breathing and saturated with thought, Dante
> understood as the beginning of prosody . . . the

metrical foot is the inhalation and exhalation of the step,

and when Robert Bly says that Antonio Machado's "poetry secretes in itself the rhythm of the walker," it may be that such claims apply more directly to poets writing out of a syllabic tradition, itself derived from the original classical quantitative meter, than to someone like myself whose metrical home base, the original Anglo-Saxon meter, is accentual, where the syllables can be allowed to run wild between accents, irrespective of duration. Spanish, as I understand it, observes stress *and* syllable as a unit of measure in poetry, but that challenging complication lies beyond the boundaries of my present thinking.

The rhythm of walking, then, as I experience it in all its syllabic regularity, grounds what goes on rhythmically above it and acts in some sort of subliminal consort with it. There is a symbiosis. Leaving aside yet another vast matter, that of brain waves, one can say that the primary rhythms above the feet are those of the heart and of the breath.

The heartbeat speeds up with exercise, but its basic rhythm is iambic—*lub DUB*. The diastolic *lub* is the flowing (inhalation) of the fresh blood into the left atrium from the lungs and into the right atrium from the whole body; the systolic *DUB* is the contraction of the heart muscle and the exhalation of blood from the ventricles. As in breathing, the inhalation period tends to be longer than the exhalation and, in this regard, the heart rhythm could conceivably be thought of as anapestic—xx/—if one thinks merely in terms of duration (there is no question of where the intensity of stress occurs—in the second sound, the DUB). On a recent walk, I counted a hundred and ten steps to the minute and wondered if that rate might conceivably be either in synchronization with, or counterpoint to, my heartbeat, which might just be a hundred and ten also. Not being a physiologist, I don't know the answer to my speculation, and I don't need to know, but I am aware of many possible permutations of rhythm, all of which the walker experiences subliminally, which the act of walking sets in motion.

To add to the syllabics of walking and the iambics of the heartbeat, there is the breathing above it. The breathing seems to me to be quantitative in a rhythmical, not a metrical, sense; there are no feet in the lungs. By that I mean, simply, long or short. In meditative circumstances, say, breathing can be more under our control than the heartbeat, though never wholly so, but during walking, the exhalation period, as with the heartbeat, is both a briefer and more emphatic experience than the inhalation period. It is, of course, possible to center on your breathing while walking, and even to do a specific walking meditation, but I am focusing on processes generally thought of as autonomous—that is, not under our physiological governance.

Walking, I am polyrhythmical, an intricate, self-enclosed world. Human beings are already essentially rhythmical creatures, but in motion, that intrinsic rhythmical nature is now intensified into a highly complex and varied orchestration. The landscapes of whatever kind I walk through—the species, the tribes, the varieties, the variations—surround me with their rhythms (aural, visual, olfactory, among others), and I find myself better tuned than usual, more opened, in my rhythmically charged walking state, to let them in and to be affected by them. In this collaborative circumstance, the two worlds, human and nonhuman, engage with an untypical intimacy—one possible reason for Housman's "sudden and un-accountable emotion" and for the appearance of "sometimes a line or two of verse, sometimes a whole stanza at once." This constitutes a marrying of rhythms in which, if you are in "a receptive and expectant frame of mind," the body, with its often neglected energies re-alerted and re-released by the act of walking, participates, with the result that the walker consists of a matrix of rhythms composed of body, mind, and physical surroundings (ongoing crude distinctions).

This puts the intellect in its place. This says that the indispensable intellect is not the primary agent in the writing of poetry. This reminds us that "verse," meaning "turn," has its origins in sacred dance, and that the poem is, like the body itself, a rhythmical world. This says, with Housman, the scholar of classical literature, that poetry is "more physical than intellectual." Walking might be said to compensate for habitual and excessive thinkiness, for incessant cerebration; it might put the walker more fully back in the body, a body moving across ground that itself seems inert but is actually in motion, beginning at the molecular level.

It is possible for me to go months between poems, for all the thoughts and feelings and opinions and experiences that I have during that time. What is often missing, I think, is an initiating rhythm which enables me to gather all the disparate elements together into the orbit of the poem; to walk is to invite the body into a complex of intimate relationships in which thinking, feeling, and the body's own intrinsically rhythmical nature harmonize with the landscape through which it is moving and in which it lives—and that it too often disregards.

There is never a guarantee of imaginative outcome in the act of walking, and it would be gruesome and self-conscious to see everything as grist, as potential "material"; this would be to cheapen the innate value both of looking and of walking. In recent years I have taken to walking with a little tape recorder handy, and into this I murmur, sometimes to the amusement or curiosity of neighbors or passers-by, whatever occurs to me, almost all of it occasioned by my looking. I have come to rely on this as one main way of writing—something which would have astonished the younger poet I once was—but the key element is my encounter with the immediate surroundings, what the day, moment by moment, is bringing me. I walk to walk: the act has its own value, and the words, if they happen to arrive, are in the nature of a gift—a gift I had not planned to receive.

Just as I don't know what triggered D. H. Lawrence's benign and inspired mood during his walk with Eleanor Farjeon and Edward Thomas—the company, the walking, or the whitebeams—so I don't feel able to say, finally, which of the rhythms involved in walking is the chief begetter of whatever words might occur to me. And, to say it again, I don't need to know. Instead, I set out as a walker and then rely on what happens. Alfred Alvarez has described Lawrence's poetry as a series of "improvisations at the full pitch of his intelligence." It is to just such a pitch that I believe walking brings the body, a pitch of rhythmical intelligence, and in this condition the improvisations are sometimes known to begin. May they continue.

1998

Next Year You Can See for Yourself

Paul Engle changed my life.

I'd begun reading American poetry in the early 60s, first in Helsinki, at the U.S.I.S. Library, and then back in England after my year in Finland. In poets such as James Wright, Theodore Roethke, Anne Sexton, William Stafford, W. S. Merwin, and James Dickey, to name a few, I found language and images that suggested all kinds of new possibilities to my own uncurling imagination.

In Helsinki, I'd met Chester Anderson, a Joyce expert and Fulbright Scholar at the University of Helsinki. We began a lifelong friendship in the fall of 1963 and it was Chet (best man, "best Chet," at my wedding eighteen years later) who gave me a list of American creative writing programs, with the name "Iowa" at the top. Funny-looking word, I thought: is that where the Mormons are?

Back in England in the summer of 1964, I spent some time at the American Embassy in London, reading up on creative writing programs, and made the decision to try to go to Iowa. I applied to enter the program and to support myself for two years with a teaching assistantship in French.

Late in October of 1964, I received a blue airmail letter from Paul Engle in Iowa City. The information in the letter was definitely of interest—Paul assured me of acceptance into the program and of receiving the assistantship—but the large and very scarlet maple leaf Paul had enclosed in the letter especially thrilled me—a living piece of the landscape I dreamed to enter. What also excited me were Paul's words: "Next year you can see for yourself." And so I did, as he promised. And I have an American life, thanks to him.

Over many years, Paul Engle helped thousands of people, and it's possible he sent out thousands of Iowa leaves inside blue airmail letters, but I took the gesture entirely personally—it was magic to me and has always stayed with me. It was a poet's gesture, all right.

I found in Paul's own poems, which I sought out, the kind of vigor I later saw in the man. Raised on the sonnet, I responded to the music and firmness of form of "American Child," while finding in its images intimations of a landscape different from the one I began in, vivid details of the new world that was to become my own: "Her hands are autumn when the crop is done / . . . Her hair is winter drifted with blonde snow." Minnesota has been my home for twenty-five years, and so I know about harvest and snow (and children and ducks and the north)—and also the large maple leaves, the kind that are whirling in late October as I write this.

I have two main memories of Paul. One is of his voice, utterly distinctive, some witty confluence of Iowa and Oxford, clipped, firm (like the poems), a gleam to the phrasing, a natural cadence, a warm tone. It was a welcomer's voice: it invited.

At the same time, there was something of the fencer's agility in his vocal manner—he always seemed to enjoy encountering a lithe or forthright conversationalist, someone with whom he could thrust and parry, whom he could *engage* in conversation; there was an obvious relish to the way he delivered well-turned phrases and frequent *bons mots*. There was also a mischievous and fun-loving, ever-young quality to the voice; he must have been quite a boy.

That tone and manner are well preserved in a paragraph such as this (from the introduction to *Seems Like Old Times*):

> Of course there are risks. The mild frost of a
> university air can kill the tender plant. Excess of
> self-consciousness can slow down a talent which has
> little momentum. And English novelist, V. S. Pritchett,
> laments that the American university may induce an
> unnatural hostility to vulgarity in the writer. Have no
> fear. They will not lose their vulgarity.

I read that and I hear Paul's voice. I hear, if you'll allow the synesthesia, the gleam.

My other main memory is of Paul the Great Convenor. Lord, that man loved to get people *together*—he must have had a convening gene somewhere deep inside. The Workshop and the International Writing Program were, of course, a huge convening of many years' duration.

For myself, I remember a number of early communal excursions—a football game that first fall (the enemy being icy invaders from the north, the currently reeling Golden Gophers of Minnesota), followed by a party at the house, where I discovered bourbon; an excursion to Chicago and the Playboy Club—what were we doing there? Did we go anywhere else in Chicago?; a visit to Des Moines, where we were grandly entertained in the penthouse suite of one of the patrons of the program, of the sort Paul so skillfully courted.

Even after I'd left Iowa, Paul's kindness reached me; thanks to him, I was invited to a conference at the Library of Congress in the early 70s and had the huge pleasure of sharing a platform with N. Scott Momaday, among others, and hearing Momaday recite:

Remember my horse running.
Remember my horse.
Remember my horse running.
Remember my horse.

Unforgettable.

And when I returned to Iowa City in the mid-80s to give a reading and a talk to members of the International Writing Program, a favorite memory is of a boisterous dinner in a Chinese restaurant on the outskirts of town to which Paul and Hualing had invited, oh, a few people . . .

I didn't know Paul that well, probably, finally, though I always liked him. (I was also very full of myself at the time and may have been hard to know.) My first year at Iowa was the Workshop in the huts by the river and his last as director, and I never actually took a course from him. But he made a strong impression on me, that father to so many writers, and I'll always be grateful to him.

In the week Paul died, I was visiting the James Wright Festival in Martin's Ferry, Ohio; there I had the opportunity to pay my homage to a poet who has meant so much to me. And when I heard that

Paul had died at O'Hare, between planes, as I said my prayer for him, it seemed to me that it was appropriate, somehow, for death to come to him this way—while he was still in the saddle, or had his boots on (or whichever expression might fit).

He who had told me I could see for myself is gone, but his example lives on in many writers, including myself, whom he honored at the times in their lives when they were most in need, with his untiring generosity and support. God rest him.

1999

The Poem Behind the Poem

I once found a definition of melody in a life of Beethoven: "A combination of cadence and surprise." "Cadence" comes from the Latin *cadere*, to fall, and although it means something a little different for the composer than for the poet—it more nearly suggests closure—still, by this definition, we can picture both melody and phrase as something rising a while which then begins to fall, only to be lifted or infused with new life at a point where it begins to drop.

I want to talk about one or two of the sources of that rebirth or renewal, because so many of our poems seem to me like thrown stones that return too soon to earth. To switch metaphors, they turn for home too soon. Richard Hugo suggests that a poem often has an initial subject and a generated subject, and it's my feeling that most poems fail to generate their true subjects, the subjects often implicit in their opening phrases, even as early as the title. When I'm working with a poem, my own or someone else's, which fails to fire the loaded pistol it began with (to invoke Chekhov), I often suggest going back to the early moments to see how we chose, or were invited, to begin. The beginning of a poem is seminal in terms of sound, image, rhythm, in terms of putting us on the path, often a very wandering one, to addressing what Allen Grossman calls "the authentic problem." The problem can rarely be anticipated by the poet in advance of the poem. "If I can think of it, it's not what I want," is a line in a poem by Randall Jarrell, and if a poem can be thought of as the only possible way of saying whatever it ends up saying, then it must make its discoveries as it goes—it must generate its surprises.

In Richard Wilbur's poem "The Writer," the poet listens to his daughter upstairs in the family house working on a story at the typewriter, and at the end of five stanzas he wishes her life "a lucky passage." He interprets the pause she makes at this moment as a rejection of his "easy figure"; he then spends five stanzas recreating the memory of a trapped bird's struggle to escape from that same upstairs room two years ago. After imagining/remembering the bird's final success in "clearing the still of the world," he returns to his daughter, saying "It is always a matter, my darling, / Of life or death, as I had forgotten." It's not so often that we see this mellifluous poet erupt into such plainness or risk of statement; not only does he publicly, within his own poem, call into question the glibness of his own metaphor, but he ends the poem with the kind of large terms—"life or death"—that creative writing instructors talk themselves blue in the face forbidding students to use in their poems. This ending seems to me a clear example of the poem behind the poem, and to see how Wilbur might have made this discovery. I want to go back to where he begins.

The poem's title, "The Writer," already provides some momentum toward the poem's final theme, which has as much to do with the fatherly, as with the fledgling, writer. And then the first three lines:

> In her room at the prow of the house
> Where light breaks, and the windows are tossed with
>   linden,
> My daughter is writing a story.

He doesn't begin with lines such as these:

> In her room at the front end of the house
> Where light shines, and the windows are surrounded
>   by linden,
> My daughter is working on a story.

A lot of our poems begin as palely as this, with as little sense of arousal, and a chief result of our pale word-choices is pale associative thought, pale discovery, pale progression, pale resolution. Wilbur's early choices—"prow," "breaks," "tossed"—offer, at the very least, a proposition of sound and image to his ear and his imagination; they propose an initiative of pattern and association which the poem triumphantly follows through to its end.

A poem proceeds on its sound and on its images, proceeds in strides which preclude many minor descriptive steps, descriptive delays, which are finally non-contributory; by this, I mean that tendency to cluster fattening descriptions, often in triples, causing them to dawdle or mark time while the scent fades. If a phrase can create the right richness the first time, then the poem can move on.

In this poem of Wilbur's, leaving aside such important matters such as the poem's metrical beauty and the rhythmical pattern of line-endings, which contribute strongly to the poem's effect, we can measure one sequence of strides, mainly through participles and participial adjectives: "tossed . . . shut . . . bunched . . . dazed . . . humped" and on to the final "I wish what I *wished* you before but harder." This recurrence seems to be aroused by the energized nature of the first of these sounds, "tossed," and works as a detectable verbal pulse in the piece. If you were to take a dozen colored pencils and chart the various patterns of sound and image running this poem, you would create quite a display.

I want to suggest that articulation of the authentic problem surfaces in this poem, insists itself into the final lines, because the poet takes up the proposition of sound that he offers himself, intuitively, at the poem's beginning. Language in poetry, Auden says somewhere, is not the handmaiden but the mother of thought: words release their energy to other words in poems; they call to and echo one another across the stanzas. The confrontation with turbulence, which Wilbur was avoiding early in this poem with his "easy figure," is sown there at the very beginning, with those first words; the result is that, by the sixth stanza, he becomes capable of dealing with the memory of the starling, "dazed," "humped and bloody" (inevitably we think back to "tossed" in the second line), and so he becomes capable of working through to a much deeper, more empowered, awareness of his daughter's situation and some of its meanings for him. He lets it "break" into him. Simply put, he can't deal with it at first, or he deals with it only superficially, but his own charged words propel him toward that confrontation: he rides their sounds to get there. Paler words could not accomplish such a thing—there's no proposition to them.

In *The Psychopathology of Everyday Life*, Freud uses the term "screen memory" to describe either an event in the past that we're drawn to and which leads us, by association, to an event in the present, the one which is really obsessing us but which we can't confront directly, or an event (image, object, and so on) in the present which it is screening, but which can eventually lead us to something in the past that we need to come to terms with. Perhaps this corresponds to the generation of the authentic problem out of the initial theme, the sometimes drastic swing of the compass needle which, part way through a poem, points us in a direction that our conscious intention had never considered and might even have backed away from.

Often in dealing with a poem that doesn't seem to be working, I ask, "Where's the second emotion?" I find myself saying that it takes two to parent a poem and that many of our poems seem to fail their early potential because we don't manage to generate the second emotion, or subsequent ones. One reason for that failure is the lack of charge in our words. Although the indirection of Wilbur's journey carried no guarantee that it would lead him to his final statement, he laid himself open to the possibility of such discovery by the energy of his first words and images (no space here to speak of the monumental "prow"). In a sense, we cast ourselves upon the mercy of our own process, our own linguistic and imagistic inventing when we set out into a poem. The results, all in Wilbur's poem seem to me permanently stirring.

In Sharon Olds' poem "Prayer During a Time My Son is Having Seizures," an initially weak parent becomes empowered by the poem's end, and rises memorably to an occasion which, at the poem's beginning, provokes feelings of impotence. The poem opens: "Finally, I just lean on the door-frame, a / woman without belief, praying" and ends "I'll change his dark radiant diapers . . . I will have him on any terms." How does the helpless leaner of the first line straighten to sit stoically, heroically, in the final lines? It is less because of this poem's sound, I suspect, although those first lines have a quantity of it, and more because of the ferocity of naming through image, which proceeds from the first "lean," the poet's own stance, through a succession of fearsome pictures in which she imagines her susceptible son falling (four times), darkening, being lopped, being hit, sliding, being pushed off a high wire, having his toys (thoughts) ripped away, drooling, and more. This unprecedented stream of visions takes up the imagistic proposition of the first lines in ways that surely overwhelmed the poet herself. What she comes to in her poem, what she generates by entering the arena of her vilest fears, is poetic statement of a resonance that must have been unthinkable before she actually started in on the words. As it does in Wilbur's poem, the screened, authentic problem is transformed into utterance which from now on will be dissolved into the poet, will become a part of who she is and how she sees the world. There is no mistaking the force of such discoveries; they cannot be faked, and there is no going back from them.

1988

The Duty of the Moment

The Sorrow

What is asked of us at this time is that we feel the sorrow of the terrible events. Nazim Hikmet, the Turkish poet, in his poem "On Living," considers the extinction of the earth and says: "You must grieve for this right now / you have to feel this sorrow now." Adrienne Rich, in conversation with us just last week, suggested that we have to "absorb the sorrow into our cellular structure." Bad political poetry, she went on to say, comes from a lack of absorption in the sorrow.

Robert Bly, in his essay "Leaping up into Political Poetry," claims that the strongest poetry written in America during the Vietnam War came from those who had first mapped out the complexities of their own inner lives in a serious and sustained way (he calls them "inward poets"): If that kind of ongoing inner work is not done first, then the writing and thinking that result tend to be emptily rhetorical. What are we hearing from our present leadership and from many of our fellow citizens but the rhetoric of the exclusively angered? Is anger appropriate in the face of the present evil? Of course it is: great evil has been done. But first, for us, the sorrow, in all its immensity—to feel the grief of the desperate whose loved ones are gone, instantly invisible; the grief of the exhausted rescuers digging in the rubble; our own grief as we contemplate the unthinkably changed world that is our duty of the moment. "We make out of the quarrels with others, rhetoric," writes Yeats, "out of the quarrels with ourselves, poetry."

Hope

"You can't tell the children there is no hope." Our family of five gathered together the evening of September 11 to talk of the tragedy and to listen to one another, and my contribution to the discussion was to remind the children of some of the stages they

131

go through—how they learn, over time, that parents are flawed and far from god-like; how their parents (and other relatives) die and disappear from life; how they experience events that parents cannot protect them from, such as this present nightmare—and to say, as a consequence of these realities, that we must love one another, live in whatever time we have together at the deepest levels of our being, faithful to demanding reality, re-dedicate ourselves to true kindness, real compassion, values we try to live by and, all too often, falter in carrying through.

Thirteen weeks ago, my sister Angela died. I have been rocked by that death, bruised by that death, and also, as she would want me to—she would insist!—I have been living in hope—in resurrection and the life to come, which is our family's faith—and inspired by the example of the intensity and loving radiance of her life (a life cut short, but a life at once fully aware of the sufferings of the world and also lived in hope).

As we dig in the rubble, as we lose heart, as we break down, as we fail to be eloquent, as we make fools of ourselves, as doubts pour in, as we don't measure up to some unrealistic standard of composure, as we are shaken by the sorrow, as we despair, we must also try allowing the hope to live its life in us, somehow, somehow, drawing on whatever sources we can manage, leaning on whatever arms can continue to be strong for us.

Language

To moan, to gulp, to gasp, to weep, to pant, to blurt, to keen, to howl, to yell, to shout, to scream, to rant, to bellow, to caterwaul, to lament—how do we bring such sounds into our language without excessive self-consciousness? When my father Eddie was declared dead, over forty years ago, Angela, twenty-one years old, howled so hard amid the April blossoms that the porter at the English hospital came out from his little front office to check on the dog that was obviously in pain. I have yet to write that howl. Whatever is asked of us, we need to seek out language as extreme, as risky as possible, that utters it, not least to give others the opportunity to

be there, to feel it and experience all its resonances.

Susan Griffin writes: "Each time I write, each time the authentic words break through, I am changed . . . I follow language. I follow the sounds of the words, and I am surprised and transformed by what I record."

What is asked of us is that we try to say, to take the measure the event, to go in search of syllables or let them come to us (in dreams, in fevers, in states of contemplation), to sweat in the rubble of whatever our situation is, to witness. Writing can be transformative, as Susan Griffin says, and, like prayer, while it does not cause disappeared people (or destroyed buildings) to rise again in our sight, it can, on occasion, allow what was most alive in them to live on through rhythms and images supposedly of our own making—every piece of writing being, of course, a wholly collaborative act (are we ever less alone than when we write?). *Ubi sunt qui ante nos fuerunt?* Where are those who were here before us? In our language, in our words, our poems, stories, essays, articles, songs, if we can learn, by practice—more ongoing work—how to have them speak (or howl or curse or bless, or all of these) by way of us. "Poets exist so that the dead may vote," says Elie Wiesel. And *we* must vote, charged by their example.

My Foe

We can choose vengeance, "become what we hate," permit the slaughter of innocents ("collateral damage"). What does that make us? Blake's poem "A Poison Tree" ends with the speaker's empty victory "In the morning glad I see / My foe outstretched beneath the tree." The enemy who stole from him and ate the poisoned apple from the tree that he (the poet) watered with his fears, now lies there in all the pathos of his lifeless body. Is that what we want?

I can't say I know what we should do; born just after World War II began, I would have served in that conflict, if born twenty years earlier, against a discernible and very real enemy. But I would have said, and say, "No" to Dresden and the fire bombing, "No" to

Hiroshima and Nagasaki. According to the principles of the "just war," out of my own faith tradition, you cannot undertake aggression if the resulting destruction is to be out of proportion to what was sustained, and you cannot ever intend harm to the innocent. All around us, we hear calls for death to the aggressor (whoever it may be) without any counting of the cost. It is not possible, I believe, to allow the sorrow "into our cellular structure," into the depths of our ethical being, and be able to make such calls; when I hear them, I think of what the Duke of Wellington is reported to have said as his own dragoons marched by on the eve of the battle of Waterloo—"I don't know if they frighten the enemy, but by God, they frighten me." And I think of Camus' "I would like to be able to love my country and still love justice."

The Duty of the Moment

The title phrase, in this piece of echoes, is not mine—it is from Catherine Doherty, a Russian-born Canadian who founded the Madonna House community in Ontario, an activist organization which now has "field houses" world-wide, feeding, teaching, sheltering those in need. In her brief essay "The Duty of the Moment," her thoughts are similar to those from writers of various areas of belief I have read over the years, many of them Zen/Buddhist (Charlotte Joko Beck, Thich Nhat Hahn, Gary Snyder, Ram Dass, Jack Kornfield, John Tarrant, among others) as well as thinkers such as Thomas Merton and Thomas Keating out of Doherty's own Christian tradition.

Catherine Doherty tells us that whatever we do, however small the task, however tedious or unpalatable, we need to do it mindfully, with full awareness: changing a diaper, sweeping the floor—"Whatever your duty is, you do it with great love." It is an old lesson; it is a profound one. And loving one's "neighbor," often such a task, and one daily asked of us, stands at the center of the system of belief she lives by. No use to cry, "Lord, Lord," says the scripture, if you are not loving, forgiving, loving, forgiving. At our family meeting last week, I was trying to talk about that—how, moment by moment, we need to be fully present to one another, faithful to the moment, we whose names are "writ in water," and, beyond us, present to to our community and communities, to the suffering world at large.

Here are the last lines of something Angela wrote in the spring of this year, a month or two before her death, a prayer / poem found in a drawer in her home in England:

> I desire to be ALL LOVE.
> To chuck out all the selfish, egotistical rubbish
> and give give give joy to those I love,
> and those I don't love! Yet.

Each of us has a sense of how many there are we don't love— yet—all those unpalatable neighbors, acquaintances, colleagues, factions, races, nations—and, quite possibly, our own selves, parts of our selves, which is where the trouble often, unconsciously, begins. So many parts of ourselves are disowned, seem unacceptable to us—and, by projection, aspects of so many who are not us. The duty of the moment, the grievous, grievous moment, in all its enormity, lies before us.

September 17, 2001

Words for Music

Writing words for music is like building a boat rather than a house—you want something firm, buoyant, that will float when the music arrives. Build too heavy, and things sink. (And most words for music on the page are about as interesting as boats on sand.)

You leave room for the music. The main job of any text written for music, poetry or prose, is to release the composer's shaping spirit—the words, like those of a poem on the page, being an opportunity for their reader (in this case, the composer) to imagine. Working with words, I start by pulling structures, some of them very free indeed, from out of my own world of shapes, and offer them toward the music. This involves huge amounts of play, lots of eventually unusable material—if it occurs to me, I write it down—until, at usually some late stage in the process, a vision of order begins to suggest itself. At that point, I am drawing upon patterns from anywhere that may be of help—from what I love and know in poetry, prose, painting, music, landscape, and the like—until at last the work is, if not finished, at least ready to show to the composer. Then come, typically, discussions, revisions, re-revisions, bargainings, dismemberments even. The text for music is always provisional.

I have no idea how "my" composers do what they do, and have often been astonished by what they have been able to make out of the sometimes very informal possibilities I have proposed to them. Recitative-like language can become, by some miracle of art and craft, aria-like music; gleaming veins of musical formality can appear in verse I had thought was, in essence, "free."

On occasion, the music comes first—the roles are reversed and a whole other set of challenges comes into play. This is a relatively rare circumstance, but some of my favorite experiences have been when I set out to try to find some words worthy of an outstanding melody—for Stephen Paulus' "Pilgrims' Hymn," for example, or

"As a River of Light" by John Foley S.J. While I'm likely to tremble at such a challenge, I also relish the opportunity—I bring everything I have in me to bear on the task.

And it is in such situations—when something formal, such as a repeated melody with metrically identical stanzas, tends to be involved—that I get closest to my favorite forms of music, the hymn and the carol—the latter generally the pre-modern kind, as in "Lullay My Liking, My Dear One, My Sweeting"; "There Comes a Ship A-Sailing"; "I Sing of a Maiden That Is Makeless"; "Balulalow"; and the like—and to write words which, though not pastiche, are my own form of reverence toward the spirit of those sprightly, tender sounds. As a non-musician, I also enter into a deep kind of connection with my long-dead father, my organist, choirmaster, pianist, singer, English father, whom still, though I am now older than he was able to be, I hunger after.

Then there is the matter of harmony, that magical simultaneity of effect for which composers are quite rightly the envy of verbal artists (see, for example, Ezra Pound's notion of the image as a "visual chord"). In the presence of harmony, I find my appetite for life, my inclination to *make something*, enhanced to an unusual degree. "From harmony, from heavenly harmony, this universal frame began," says the poet John Dryden. I believe him.

I'm not sure how guilty a pleasure this is, if it is one at all; I take courage, as it were, from D.H. Lawrence's revealing essay "Hymns in a Man's Life" or Elizabeth Bishop's choice of seven hymns as "poetry of a kind, I am fairly sure," in the fall 1971 is-sue of the Academy of American Poets' *Poetry Pilot*, and it can be fascinating to trace the influence on certain very free-spirited, free form poets of some very formal and traditional sources—of Blake on Allen Ginsberg, say, or Chaucer on Philip Levine.

One large difference between words in poems and words written for music is the size of the audience involved. As a librettist, from the start I am not "someone alone in a room with the English language," as Berryman describes the poet; rather, I am part of a team, not my own boss, something of a second fiddle—and I relish (that's that word again) the happily subordinate role.

And when—to take one example—"Pilgrims' Hymn" was sung at Orchestra Hall in Minneapolis recently, at the "Elegy" concert commemorating the tragedies of September 11, sung by a combined choir of three hundred voices, to an audience of perhaps two thousand and, beyond them, to a national radio audience, I was very aware that in the service of music, words of mine can reach many more people—unprecedented numbers of them—than those my books of poems, with their very modest visibility, are able to. With sales of this piece over the first four years of its life approaching twenty thousand, and with its inclusion in already a dozen CDs, Stephen and I have the sense that this hymn has truly entered the repertory and is finding its way into people's lives in the way that only music, even only songs of a certain kind, can do. (It is not a matter of sales and statistics for me, of course, but of a different kind of belonging.)

How do I feel about this? And how do I feel about these boats of mine, this "poetry of a kind," as Bishop calls it? Well, I feel lucky, for one thing. I feel lucky beyond any deserving, for the company and friendship of the composers I have worked with, Stephen Paulus and John Foley principally, and for what I have learned in the many dialogues that our collaborations have involved. The writing I have done I see as worthy, overall, and in harmony with the writing I have done for the page (though it is always my hope that the poems will be taken off the page and heard as speech, the most musical speech I can manage). While there are only a very few pieces I have written for music that I might ever recite at a reading as poetry, I view them all with a certain fondness as, to use Plato's term, my "mental children," though some of them live very far away now and don't get back to me too often. To have been able to contribute in this way, so that the words, married to the music they were written for, are sung in churches, temples, concert halls, school gymnasiums, studios—and may, some of them, be sung for even a considerable time to come—is more privilege and luck than I could ever have hoped for when I first set out on my life as a writer.

In my most recent collaboration with Stephen Paulus, earlier this year, I was asked to come up with words for an exquisitely touching melody, "Prospect," from the Southern Harmony collection of 1833, for which Stephen had been commissioned to create a new arrangement. After first talking with Stephen about the overall mood of the piece, and some possible themes, I lived with the melody for several weeks, singing it to myself over and over, trying out many many phrases and combinations of phrases, cutting and pasting and discarding, and had several further lively, detailed discussions with Stephen, usually about drafts I had sent or brought to him, both of us (writing partners, on and off, since 1976) working to achieve the significant simplicity we felt this music required. Here are the words we came to for the third and final verse of "The Road Home," sung, in performance, in four-part harmony with a solo soprano descant:

> Rise up, follow me,
>> Come away, is the call,
> With the love in your heart
>> As the only song;
> There is no such beauty
>> As where you belong:
> Rise up, follow me,
>> I will lead you home.

You would not hear this from me at a poetry reading, but it's a great tune, and I long to sing it.

2001

Something Stood Still in My Soul

"The moment I saw the brilliant, proud morning
shine high up over the deserts of Santa Fe, something
stood still in my soul, and I started to attend."

D. H. Lawrence, a very great poet and a very anxious Englishman, encountered something in New Mexico that slowed him down—slowed him to the point of causing something in his soul to stand still. He wrote: "I think New Mexico was the greatest experience from the outside world that I have ever had. It certainly changed me forever."

When I remember what Lawrence said, I always also think of William Blake, and two of my favorite proverbs from *The Marriage of Heaven and Hell*; one says: "When thou see'st an Eagle, thou see'st a portion of Genius; lift up thy head!" And the other: "Eternity is in love with the productions of time." It's strange, perhaps, to think of an eagle as a "production of time," but ever since Blake, I always do: its wings, amazing as they are, are of this world. And by that one fact, they make this world amazing. (Of New Mexico, Lawrence also wrote: "What splendour! Only the tawny eagle could really sail out into the splendour of it all.")

The new world landscape of New Mexico had that eagle genius for Lawrence. It made him begin to pay attention—to be, as he says elsewhere, "a man in his wholeness, wholly attending." ("Woman," I would also want also to say.) Again and again, in imaginative literature, in books and teachings on meditation and centering prayer and spirituality, we read of such exchanges—moments when, through attentiveness, we come to glimpse, and even sometimes experience, a changed way of being in the world. What is it that happens? We go from our usual condition, one in which we are neither here nor there—scurrying and spiraling, spinning, toppling, fluttering, despairing, losing hold, losing heart, far from any nest—and there comes upon us an experience of blessedness, a sense, however transitory, of being steeped in confidence in the universe. It is, perhaps, like what the poet Paul Eluard means when he writes: "There is another world. It is inside this one." Or Gerard Manley Hopkins: "There lies the dearest freshness deep down things." The cause may be a landscape, as it was in this case for Lawrence, or the consequence of a consistent spiritual practice such as meditation, but it is, essentially, unbidden. It comes, or it does not come. It is "like a pool into which we plunge / or do not plunge," as Lawrence says in a poem. First, and always, the stillness, as a pre-condition of whatever may come—including, perhaps, a sense of the divine presence. "Be still," says the scripture," and know that I am God."

When I have been working with a student for a number of years and we are about to part company and s/he asks me for advice, typically I will say: "Keep good company." For the purposes of today's sessions, I would say that the present moment is the very best company we can keep, and learning to be *in* it, to enter fully into it with our alert but relaxed attention, is the most beneficial practice possible, both spiritually and poetically. And it does *take* practice, this reverencing of life, this homage to its moment by moment by moment. Like Mary, we sit at the feet of the moment with our attentiveness, while our busy Martha mind has other tasks for us and likely fusses in the background, obliged to wait—not too happy with us.

And if, as a writer, I am to make actual poetry, some articulation that may cross from my own life into the lives of others, then the unbidden also is the case: we can expect nothing. As in the advice of the great Thich Nhat Hahn, we must wash the dishes—the words, the syllables, the rhythms, the images—to wash them, for their own sake, for the doing of it, not with thoughts of getting them clean; we do it to do it, never to have it done. The process has its own wisdom and will, or will not, generate something beyond itself in language. What I must first do is pay attention to the moment, to the genius of the landscape of language, for its own genius self.

The advice on this subject from so many sources, advice on

the wisdom of this way of proceeding, seems so consistent, that it is almost amusing to see the resistance we put up to the practicing of stillness. It may be that our own encounters often take place, typically, in far less dramatic circumstances than Lawrence's—in the sound of freeway traffic, perhaps, and with just ten or twelve minutes to spend before leaving to drive a child to school or walking the dog or going to work—whatever it is the reality of our lives is asking of us. No eagles; no arroyos.

But the possibility, wherever we are, remains the same: we begin to go below the day and into another sense of time. We become aware, we focus on the breathing, the miraculous reliable breathing; we are present to that also, perhaps even for the whole duration of our sitting. On occasion, we can be brought to awareness of some unutterably deep *with-us*, the nameless, nearer to us than we are to ourselves, to whose presence we consent by being there in silence. None of our usual agendas, our Martha-ness, will bring us there.

And yet, for all these riches, the resistance is there. Jack Kornfield says it brilliantly: "The mind dismisses the present moment." And again, he says: "Our first task is to get here"—suggesting, I think, that we have to work at it. Something in us wants anything at all than to be present to each moment. We "study to be quiet." John Tarrant, another exceptional teacher of Zen, often ends a teaching (this from my reading only) with: "Each moment full and complete." That is the goal: faithful mindfulness. It can be so rare, for most of us, and yet we can put up such resistance—or somebody in us does—to the possibilities of the experience. "Why do we live so much not here?" Jack Kornfield asks.

For myself, when I falter, which is often—it is certainly a "moment faith" I live by—I take courage from writings that describe these states and struggles familiar to me. Where would I be without these poems, these prayers, these meditations? I carry them with me. Lao Tzu, writing in China around 600 BCE, speaks of connecting the mind with "the subtle origin" until, calmed, it becomes "as vast and immeasurable as the night sky."

Could this be the same subtle origin whose presence Lawrence felt in the new world, that made his soul stand still? Whether or not it is so, what a miracle it is, this act of attention toward what is not the mind, what is not the anxiety, what is not the projection, what is not the fantasy, what is not the incessant interpreting interpreting interpreting we all do—what Charlotte Joko Beck, yet another great Zen teacher, calls the thought-feeling barrier. What we attend to, what invites us into stillness, does not have its origins with us but is, rather, the bounty of reality, an intrinsic generosity of being, of limitless depths that we are born to and intended for, but which we experience too fitfully. We let the world take it away from us little by little, we allow ourselves to be closed down, governed by our habits and not our acts of attention, our mindfulness of each moment and its possibilities, which can bring, as Wordsworth writes of "the meanest flower that blows," "thoughts that do often lie too deep for tears." It lies deep; we need to practice our going and being there.

There is genius in the moment. There is genius in each object, each element of creation. "If we could understand the rose," says Wittgenstein, "we could understand the universe." Wordless, the Buddha holds up the flower. Christ calls us to consider the lilies. Only contemplation of them can begin to suggest the depths in which they have their being, which is potential in us. I think of painters, who cannot leave the light alone, cannot leave the landscape alone, who return to it again and again in all conditions of light, again and again to the human face, the human figure, the bowl of fruit or the vase of flowers on the table or the table itself or the grain of the wood of the floor. All subject matter is sufficient, for painter, for poet, given to us as it is by the genius of the divine imagination, however disguised it may seem to us in the world as we wander in it, glazed over by our inattentiveness. By consistent practice, it is possible for us to turn our habitual useless anxiety into attention, our default fear into the deepest experience of blessedness and presence.

Bede Griffiths, whom I think of as a Benedictine pioneer, describes how we live on the surface of our being, and of how we can "lose the sense of time and enter into a deeper region of the soul," an inner sanctuary, center or ground of being, where "the soul is at all times in direct contact with God." This does not disparage the senses. It does not disparage imagination or intellect; it puts them in their place, as threshold elements, as entrances to what lies within and beyond the anxiously interpreting self. Poets, like painters, necessarily love the things of the world—signs, symbols, tropes, figures, syllables, meters, devices and recurrences of all kinds—all the while knowing that the ground of reality is not that, not that— *neti, neti*—none of these things we necessarily love so well.

It is complex, this love of what thrives, blazes up, what does not last—those things that are of the world but, like the wings of the eagle, suggest worlds beyond themselves. This is the way of the *via positiva*: the palpable beauty and weight of things, that invite us, by our attention to them, to descend below the day, below secular time, and dwell there, for at least some while; there we may, on occasion, sense the changeless one who dwells in us, spirit poured out, moment by moment, upon the world, both within and without.

In everything we do, we are sustained by the love of God—the Maker, the Lover, the Keeper, in the language of Julian of Norwich— by whose genius of imagination the humble hazelnut is "all there is." In the most profound conditions of attention, the world as poem is revealed to us by way of its most supposedly ordinary objects, its "meanest flowers," which often we hurry by. This hurrying ungrounds us, pulls us away from hope and into states of being where the old despair, in Yeats' phrase, can call whatever it wants to us and so undo us.

I'll end with a poem by Keats:

When I have fears that I may cease to be,
Before my pen has gleaned my teaming brain,
Before high-pilèd books, in charactry,
Hold, like rich garners, the full-ripened grain.
When I behold, upon the night's starred face,
Huge cloudy symbols of a high romance,

And think that I may never live to trace
Their shadows with the magic hand of chance.
And when I feel, fair creature of an hour,
That I shall never look upon thee more,
Never have relish in the fairy power
Of unreflecting love. Then on the shore
Of the wide world I stand alone and think,
Till love and fame to nothingness do sink.

*"A Senseable God" conference, St. John's
University, Collegeville, MN. October 2004.*

What the Poem Wants

The poem we just said together was "The Delight Song of Tsoai-Talee" by N. Scott Momaday. Ezra Pound says that "literature is news that stays news." I could hear those lines, those images, every day of my life, and receive something from them. And I enjoyed the choral sound of your voices.

The poem wants you **intuitive**.

I like what Thoreau says: "The learning of a whole academy will not fashion one good line." If I think to myself—"well, let's see, I've been teaching poetry for a long time, I know a lot of poems, I know a lot about poetry, I'm a professor, I'm quite smart, let's see now, a poem; yes, this should be pretty good"—if that's my starting point, I'm in trouble. (I'm too conscious—and much too solemn, self-serious.)

I like what Carl Jung says: no one ever sat down and said, "Now, I will make up a symbol." As the ground puts forth its flowers, he says, so the psyche puts forth its symbols. One of my favorite stories about the writing of a poem comes from A.E. Housman, not only a poet with a great ear but also the greatest classical scholar and translator of his time, who, for the writing of a particular poem, he tells us, relied on what he called an involuntary process, a slightly woozy walk on Hampstead Heath after lunch to get it going—afternoons being, as he confesses, the least intellectual portion of his life. Two stanzas floated in during the walk—bubbling up from his stomach, he tells us. Maybe the third stanza came "with a little coaxing after tea," but the fourth one did not come: "I had to turn to and compose it myself," he says, "and that was a laborious business. I wrote it thirteen times and it was more than a twelvemonth before I got it right." This frank account doesn't disregard the intellect; it simply puts it in its place in the process.

But my favorite description of how the imagination works comes from Ingmar Bergman, the Swedish film director, who once said this: "I throw a spear into the darkness; that is intuition. Then I must send an army to try to locate the spear; that's intellect." What do you think? I think it's wonderful. I like the idea of the physicality of the throwing, the motion almost for its own sake. It's a little different from Coleridge's idea of "a more than usual state of excitement together with a more than usual state of order," which is a simultaneous polarity, or Novalis' notion that "art is chaos shimmering behind a veil of order," which is magnificently evocative, but Bergman's formulation has you primarily active, even wild, flinging your spears, not at all sure of where they are going, and only later sending the intellect to try to find them.

After this playfulness typically follows what I call a vision of order, in which you begin to make some decisions about what you think you want in the poem, a process in which memory has a large role, in which your love of poetry and many other kinds of structures, your sense of craft, your powers of shaping, all have a large part to play—and I will soon be talking about these things. But I like the initiating (procreative) wildness. I like to be wild as long as I need to be (and that stage may last weeks, months, or years). The day I lose my capacity for wildness, whatever my age as an artist, I'm also in trouble. "The only beautiful things," says André Gide, "are those that madness dictates and reason writes." Writing, I tell my students, should be daring. Lord, let me not lose my wildness.

If the poem wants you intuitive, then it wants you improvising. "Improvise" breaks down into "im-pro-viṣore," which means "not foreseen," I love the poetry of D.H. Lawrence, and Alfred Alvarez describes Lawrence's poems as "improvisations at the full pitch of his intelligence." I think that's hugely helpful and accurate. When you're inspired—not a word we toss around too much these days—when you're being breathed into, that means that at the time, as Auden says, you don't quite know what you're doing. You don't have to, you don't have to be in full control: you are being intuitive, hurling spears. You probably won't find most of them later. That's what notebooks are for. Behind any book I publish are dozens of notebooks filled with unfound spears.

Gertrude Stein says that a main thing she learned from William James at Harvard was to "exclude nothing." I see the early drafts of a poem as an open audition in the imagination, where any idea or image, whether or not it can hold a tune, feels free to stand up there on the blank page, gesturing, to try out to be in the production. Keats has a famous formulation, which sees the poet as "capable of being in uncertainties, mysteries and doubts without any irritable reading after fact and reason." You need to be able to be in that condition as long as necessary, with a high tolerance for ambiguity and messiness, with no rush for closure. I like what Goethe tells us: "Do not hurry, do not rest."

For myself, I have written so many bad pages on my way to what I hope are some good poems. If ever you went into my papers in the archives at the University of Minnesota, where they are gradually being stored, boxes upon boxes, you would find many improvisations, many stops-and-starts, experiments which went nowhere; lots of dead ends. I like what Marvin Bell says: "The business of being a writer is being less and less embarrassed about more and more." (Rather than the other way round.)

Another thing I tell my students: I don't mind being wrong. I mean this about what I say in the classroom as well as what I put onto the page in draft after draft. In class, sometimes, when the disagreement is strong—even, on occasion, heated—I suggest we take the argument out into the parking lot, storm out and settle the issue right then, once and for all. That has yet to happen, I should say, but I like the empty threat: "Out in the parking lot." It defuses tensions. In many situations concerning the imagination, we need to get beyond the duality of right or wrong.

Most questions concerning poetry are, finally, to be lived, as Rilke says in his *Letters to a Young Poet*. If you were given the answer, Rilke suggests, you couldn't handle it. And if there are answers, which sometimes there may be, so many of them are in the nature of "both . . . and" rather than "either . . . or," which is another duality to get beyond. You can encounter in the teaching of poetry, as well as in certain areas of politics, or religion, what I call horrendous certainty. Roland Barthes warns us, by way of the example of Orpheus, not to turn to look at the question we are leading out of the dark toward the light of a meaning; all you end up with, he says, if you turn and look, is "a named meaning, which is a dead meaning." By such turning and looking, Orpheus once again lost his love to the darkness.

I want to go back to intuitiveness. Back to Jung's idea of the conscious intention to "make up a symbol." Working in the schools, as I have many times over the years, as well as teaching undergraduate and graduate classes, I have done all kinds of writing exercises with students of all ages, and some of them are quite silly at their point of departure: it's what I call "playing in a serious zone." Any of the issues that a student's poems come to deal with, begin to be able to deal with, can be, often are, deeply serious. But the conscious approach does not work, at least for me; I have better luck with the playful, the indirect. At the start, the compass needle can be pointing in a direction opposite to the one in which the poem will eventually go. Sometimes it's as if the beginning poet stands with arms outstretched and intones: "O great theme, come into my poem!" Well, that's not how you make symbols either.

Here's what I might do with my students—and I always do it myself, write with them, and read what I have written—start us on some little rhythmical repetitive task, maybe based on a refrain in a poem by Nadia Tueni or Tadeusz Rozewicz or Scott Momaday (our opening poem, which reveals the phrase "I am"), and as we work with the repetition, in almost a mantra-like way, it's just possible that, on occasion, a theme of some size, way down in the unconscious of the writer, may begin to rise up a little to see what is happening on the surface, lured there by the playfulness. Lures, in poetry as in fishing, tend to be colorful.

The poem should irrigate, not flood, the reader. That channeling takes craft, takes control, a steady hand. If you just dump a large quantity of water onto desperately dry ground, it will leach away fast. But you need something to pour down those channels, you need something whose nature is flowing, and you need to keep it coming in measures of your choice.

I'm talking analogically about water. Fire is, of course, a famous analogy for what takes place inside the imagination, and stealing fire from the gods is, of course, an ancient trope, if not one we favor much now. I've been teaching poetry for somewhat over four decades, writing it for more than five, and I still seek fire, in myself and in others. I want the sparks to be running through the world. I like a good blaze of language. And I like what Robert Penn Warren said quite some years ago about the contemporary scene in poetry: "There's a lot of talent around, but not much fire."

Everyone, I believe, can do these little initiating tasks, these repetitions I just spoke of. The poem wants you **playful**, so that you can go into surprising or even frivolous places without the embarrassment Marvin Bell speaks of. Good writing, I tell my students, comes, at least in part, from confidence in your subject matter; whatever it will take to get you down into the archives of memory and imagination, it's my experience that something may be dislodged at the time which, even much later, with labor and craft on your part, can begin to bear fruit as imaginative expression. Down there in the unconscious are things that you alone know, many of which you have forgotten or repressed; down there you become acquainted, or reacquainted, with the largeness, the scope, the strangeness of those contents—and it's often like actual dreams, with their extreme wildness and vivid indirectness of meaning, their sometimes savage parades, as Rimbaud called them.

I often think of Hamlet, and what he says to the Player King: "Can you play 'The Murder of Gonzago?'" "Aye, my Lord." Dreams are like players that come to the midnight castle of the mind, and their performance there, an autonomous, intuitive process, can dramatically unlock things that the conscious mind is unaware of, or is threatened by and has discarded or disowned. Poems need such dramas to be displayed for the reader by day, on the page, and I believe an artist's daily practice, in any medium, develops the capacity to hear little suggestions from within and from without, more often murmured than shouted, which have the potential to lead us somewhere we have been needing to go and not been aware of it.

You may overhear or mishear a conversation on a bus; the smell of coffee can suddenly bring back memories of a lost time; you stumble as you step into the street and up comes an image from a urgent but forgotten dream; or, as you are crossing the street, someone hurries by who reminds you of your mother, a woman dining alone at a restaurant (seen over your companion's shoulder) reminds you of your much-mourned sister; you hear an old song or hymn on the radio, one not heard since childhood. . . . Here, in Dublin, I think of the ending of Patrick Kavanagh's lovely poem in which an old man on the street seems to be saying to the poet, "I was once your father."

You must be open to it all, watching, listening, alert to what is in front of you, around you and within you, and constantly, as Eliot says, "amalgamating disparate experiences." Hard to imagine an animal in a forest who is not alert. Are we not in a forest? (A forest of symbols, Baudelaire would say.) And what kind of animal are we? Are we animal-like enough? And where is our intuitiveness in all this?

I've said that the poem wants you playful. It also requires you to work, and I'll run those two together, as I do sometimes in a workshop called "The Work and Play of the Poem." A poem can be a lot of work, a lot of practice, an extraordinary amount, and all that layering, all that trial and error, is hidden from the very one who is doing it. I like Maurice Ravel's account of writing the slow movement of the G major piano concerto: "That flowing phrase! How I worked over it bar by bar! It nearly killed me!"

How often we must "labor to be beautiful," as Yeats has it, but the work is essentially hidden, as is the playfulness. My old friend Chester Anderson, of blessed memory, a scholar of Irish literature, most especially Joyce but also Yeats, said to me once that when you look at the early drafts of some ultimately great poems by Yeats, you can see that a schoolboy could have written better at that stage, but Yeats knew that whatever was ultimately to come would come only if he allowed himself to put onto the page, in those first stages, whatever occurred to him, which later, over a long process of time, he would sift and sort. That's it, I think: you write down what occurs to you; you live with it. Anxiety for closure can almost always hurt you.

Theodore Roethke, the American poet, a favorite of mine, himself also a great lover (and sometime imitator) of Yeats, says that when you go dredging in the river, you're sure to bring up a lot of bad stuff. The unconscious is a messy place, is it not? But it's where the flowers have their roots. It is the ground of imaginative being.

Play is said to be the child's response to the world. When someone asked me once what I remembered most about my father, who died at 61 when I was 19, I said, "He was playful." My English-born father Eddie, son of a Donegal father, played the organ (also the piano, also he sang, also painted water colors). He remains for me, almost forty-eight years after his death, a model of how to be, both by play and by work, in the world.

One plays the flute, the fish, the field; why not the poem? And it was Nietzsche, I believe, who says: "I would only believe in a god who knows how to dance." Verse, *versus*, involves turns, such as the *volta* in a Petrarchan sonnet, such as the way the line itself turns; poetry has its origins in dance, sacred dance, began with movement, began with improvisation. In the conceiving and shaping of poems, they should not be stolid, these dancers of ours. Play is of their essence. They should be in motion.

The keyboard is one analogy I find myself using in the teaching of the writing of poetry: how many notes are there on your keyboard, I might ask a student, at any level of experience, and how many of them do you think you are using? I also think of the organ, and the complex combinations of stops which are possible. There are other well-known analogies—the juggler (how many apples or oranges can you keep going in the air?), or the team of horses (how many can you add to help you haul the load?)—but I find the keyboard to be the most evocative. And how many fingers are you using, I might go on to ask my student, to sound the notes in the area of the keyboard you are working in right now?

All this is presented unseverely, I should say, even playfully: every student, at any level of experience, should be given room to move, space to feel both safe and excited in. It is my job to stir up possibilities for them.

If you truly improvise, if you enter into what is not foreseen, then the situation is unprecedented, and so are its expressive possibilities (hard to stay away from *that* word). You don't know what you're getting into; you don't want to know. "If I can think of it," goes a line in a poem by Randall Jarrell, "it's not what I want." Here's a line from Theodore Roethke: "I learn by going where I have to go." And Gary Snyder quotes a painter who says "I paint what I don't know"—meaning that rather than something s/he, or the viewer, already knows.

These matters are complex, of course, and I should say that much of what we hold in our archives, and that comes forward in playfulness, has to do with memory—we feed from those deep springs. Not for nothing is Mnemosyne, Goddess of Memory, mother of the nine muses of poetry. But essentially we must—to borrow from Pound and his modernist call—"Make it new." And that requires intuitiveness, playfulness.

Let's go back to work (if we must). Sometimes you have to wrestle the poem, all night long, for weeks or months of nights. You have to persist, as Jacob did with the angel, even though the strong, wounded him. And what did Jacob say to the mysterious entity? "I will not let you go unless you bless me." The German poet Rilke, in his poem "The Man Watching" ("Die Schauende") says that in the struggle with the angel, suppose we won? That victory would make us smaller: you *want* to be defeated, he says, "decisively, by greater and greater beings." (The translation is by Robert Bly.)

There are many great poems in the language—need I tell this assembly? What a feast of reciting we could have! But there's no such thing as a total victory: the poem, as Valery famously says, is never finished, only abandoned. I have always liked descriptions of incompletion, of what we can't get our little language hands on. "Whatever we know of the world, there is always more," says a philosopher whose name I cannot remember. Adrienne Rich, in an interview, calls for larger poems. "Experience is larger than language," she says.

So we will never be done; we will never *get there*. But we "travel hopefully," we work and play at our poems, which use language, language, language, language, language, because the joys of the labor are intrinsic, and raveled in with the sweat and the frustration. There's a Buddhist saying: "You are entitled to the work but not the reward." That's a hard truth and, I think, a good one: the main reward is in the work itself, the privilege of being able to undertake the poem with all its demands, all the exertion and playfulness it requires. Fame and reputation will have to take care of themselves: we must exult in secret, as Yeats says—the most difficult thing, sometimes—for love of the labor itself.

For myself, I have written so many things people will never read (and published some I wish they had not). I have written a novel for children, for example, a task from which I learned so much, written it sixteen times, and it's likely that no one will ever read it. Well, OK. (That's what Ernesto Cardenal writes in his elegy for Thomas Merton, how he reacted when he learned of the death, in Cambodia, of his mentor: "I just said, OK." Cardenal's poem, I should add, does go on for many pages after that.) But what an involving joy it was for me, that extended story for children, what a playground it was, how much I learned from that wrestling, that why-notting, how many more notes on the keyboard I feel I was able to reach and sound by way of it.

No energy is wasted if it is given right. Years ago, I made some visits to Tom McGrath in the hospital in Minneapolis; Tom was a North Dakota-born poet who moved to Minnesota to live, eventually became ill there, and finally died there. Among his best-known works is the book-length long poem *Letter to an Imaginary*

Friend. The writing of poems was, at that late stage, beyond him, but I said to myself, as I sat there beside the very sick poet: the energy has been given; it is recorded somewhere in the universe. So if the poem wants to work, as well as play, then lucky us, I say, to have the sinew and skill to do it for as long as we can. Let us seize the day (and the night). There is no "poor me" in all this, when we fail, which is likely to be often. Well, let's be honest here, there can be, in weaker moments, which we all have; I'm sure we could all cry on one another's shoulders. But that is not the road we are on tonight. Eavan Boland has written brilliantly on the necessity of the experience of failure in a writer's life.

The poem wants you **empty**. And there may be times when the opposite is true, when it wants you full at the start, even crammed, brimming, swarming, because all useful statements and formulations about the imagination that I know of involve paradox and contradictions. They accommodate complexity. I like what William Blake says: "Without contraries is no progression." And Niels Bohr, the Danish physicist, says this: "The opposite of a correct statement is a false statement, and the opposite of a profound truth may well be another profound truth." Another nail in the coffin, perhaps, of horrendous certainty.

To me, emptiness suggests something relaxed rather than something contracted or crouched over. I think of Housman's stroll on the heath; he was filled with a nice slice of pie, perhaps, but his mind was open to whatever might choose to enter. And I associate emptiness with spaciousness. James Wright of a symphonium on Chinese poetry, said he admired that poetry for its spaciousness, its sense of what he called its "endless abundance." He felt welcome in the poems.

This story may be too well-known for me to tell, but here it briefly is: the renowned Western professor of philosophy who travels east, into the mountains, to meet a famous guru, and at that meeting, the professor talks and talks, asks and asks, interrogates and interrogates. When tea is served, the guru himself pours for the chattering professor, pours and pours until tea spills over the rim of the cup, onto the floor, and even down the steps of the room in which they are meeting. The message seems clear: what is already filled has no room in it. If you are to give, first you must be able to receive.

Once, when I was teaching a workshop on poetry and dreams, one of the writers asked: "How do we go deeper?" A huge question, of course, and my quick response was: "Practice emptying." A great deal of the spiritual writing I value also talks about emptying—about *kenosis*, about *sunyata*, "form is emptiness, emptiness is form," sometimes very challenging notions that take us out beyond our conceptual vocabulary. In an oratorio I recently wrote with the composer Stephen Paulus, which has to do with, among other things, two thousand years of anti-semitism and Christian implication in the Shoah, the Holocaust, the first line the chorus sings is this: "Create in me a great emptiness." Emptying seems a pre-requisite, somehow, for exploration, whether poetic or spiritual.

Here's a simple image of my own: sometimes your initial mental landscape, the condition of mind, heart or spirit from which you start, is filled with bristling buildings, like the skyline of a typical contemporary city; this must subside, sink out of sight, and then a cleared space appears before you, a kind of green *tabula rasa*; now new forms of life can begin to appear, fresh figures come forth, playfully manifest themselves, as in a waking dream, and we are under way with the creation of something new. It is like the morning of the world.

It's just an image, of course—a naive one, even. Coleridge says that "the poet echoes the primary imagination." I'm not going to try and tell you tonight how I believe the cosmos began, but I do think it has something to do with emptiness, the Divine alone with emptiness. Olga Broumas, a Greek-American poet, in a short prose piece called *Some Notes on Struggle and Joy*, says how much delight it is to her soul to imagine the infinite. The infinite and emptiness are not the same thing, of course, but I believe they are kin. And sometimes, when the lungs are fully emptied and then slowly, slowly begin to fill, you can have the feeling that the filling with air might have no end. No less than the capacity to breathe, and not unlike it, the capacity to imagine seems like an endowment of extraordinary symbolic resonance. And the center of many spiritual practices has to do with a focus upon breathing, a physiological activity which has almost endless associative connections.

When I begin a poem, the page is as blank for me as it is for even the most beginning writer. We are all apprentices to that emptiness, all perpetual beginners. I hope, each time, to surprise myself. I hope to be changed. I don't want to be able to predict what is coming, but I know I want it to come out of the emptiness, out of unconception, into being. Lord, let me not lose my emptiness.

The poem wants you **rhythmical**. "Rhythm" means "flow," and "meter" means "measure. Something flows in language, and you take delight in measuring it; as I said earlier, the aim is to irrigate the reader. I like what Theodore Roethke says of his remarkable, innovative "Lost Son" poems: "It's the spring and rush of the child I'm after." "Mother Goose," says Donald Hall, "is a better poet than W.H. Auden." I'm guessing he means that the rhythms are more irresistible. Auden is rhythmical, for sure, and brilliantly so, but can he match this?

> Diddle, diddle, dumpling, my son John,
> Went to bed with his britches on,
> One stocking off and one stocking on,
> Diddle diddle dumpling, my son John.

Now here's what Wordsworth would call "metrical excitement"! Or how about this?

> Here am I,
> Little Jumping Joan;
> When nobody's with me,
> I'm all alone.

In many poems, the information is along for the ride. The ride's the thing—"the roll, the rise, the carol, the creation," as Hopkins has it. I mentioned Neils Bohr just a while ago. David Bohm, another physicist, a mystically inclined one, who coined the terms "implicate order" for the inner world or worlds, and "explicate order" for the outer, suggests that a tree, say, only looks solid to us because we're seeing one frame per second, not all the other frames—sixteen or eighteen or thirty-two, however many it actually is, which are the molecular reality, if you like. We live, it seems, in a snapshot universe, one which has severe perceptual limitations, and perhaps the poet, in being innately rhythmical, is restoring complexity, is, to use another phrase from Fr. Hopkins, trying "to give beauty back to beauty's giver" by setting bundles of syllables in motion, casting onto the page, onto the explicate level, evidence of the ongoing, primarily invisible flux of the universe.

Let me give you a little bit of Hopkins: "Spring and Fall." And here's a poem by Marge Piercy, "To Be of Use," a poem less formal than the Hopkins but with an irresistible pulse to it, a piece I never tire of saying.

In such writing, which is free, not formal but definitely rhythmical, you feel yourself in the presence of a pattern of stresses. In America, William Carlos Williams and Ezra Pound wanted to modernize verse, heave the pentameter overboard, but, said Williams, "we must not lose measure." To me there's something wonderfully deceptive in poetry in that often very disparate thoughts, even outlandish associations, are bound together and borne along by the music of the flow—even in free verse, yes, absolutely in free verse, where the patterning is going on in all kinds of ways but often subliminally, below the surface.

When the rhythms of a poem are right, there's an entrancement; a spell is cast. This doesn't make the poem unreal compared with the so-called real world; the poem can open up the world from inside and reveal to us, in microcosm, and sometimes in eruptive ways, some of the amazing complexities of movement going on within it. And for myself as a writer, I can go weeks or months without a poem, weeks and months in which I have had plenty of experiences, thoughts, dreams, opinions, and all the rest of it, but there has been no initiating rhythm—no lightning strike, if you will, to set the dry grass blazing.

T.S. Eliot, who once described "The Waste Land" as just "some rhythmical grumbling," in one of his essays memorably likens the "meaning" of a poem to a piece of sirloin steak the thief takes with him when he's going to break into a house; when the breaking-in begins, and the watch dog predictably roars up, the thief hands over the meat to the dog to chomp on and be distracted by, and then goes about his business of robbing the house. The robbing is rhythmical, I think, and the meat / meaning is, as it were, a red herring. In spells, prayers, hymns, liturgies, incantations, blessings, curses, songs, lullabies, and the like, the rhythms have magical properties. And how does the Duke Ellington piece go? "Don't mean a thing if it ain't got that swing, doo wah doo wah doo wah doo wah doo wah."

The poem wants to be **itself**. It should be unlike anything you have written before: different occasions, different responses, is what I often say. We need to be various. If our poems are to have "fidelity to experience," which is what Denise Levertov asks for—and I take that to mean that they should be *like our lives*—then each moment, occasion, event, unprecedented as it is, asks of us fresh patterns, new constellations of language and thought. Writing, let me say it again, should be daring. As improvisers, it is our job to venture into what is "not foreseen." No one here tonight could say: "I'm going to be so bored by the dreams I'm going to have in the next ten years." Or: "Tonight is Friday; too bad—it's all repeats, re-runs."

Of course it has kin, this new poem which wants to be itself. It has affinities to what you have done before; inevitably, there is some of the same DNA in there. That is one more topic of true complexity. But let us say: no formulas, please; beware descriptive reflexes. At the beginning of the oratorio I have mentioned, here's another phrase the chorus sings: "Strip me of usual song." And Donald Hall speaks comically of the kind of poem he claims writing workshops in the United States turn out—the McPoem, about as distinctive as a thin, dry, mass-produced burger. I'm not saying that is fair, but it's an image that stays with you.

When I was teaching a graduate manuscript seminar one time, I collected a number of blurbs from recent collections of poetry and asked the student writers to look for some common denominators—which quality of these various poems seemed to be most praised by fellow poets and critics. The word we detected was "fresh"—freshness was, across the board, said to be the main positive quality of those writings. I believe it's Joseph Conrad who talks about the necessity of using "the fresh, usual words." There's one of the better challenges for the writer, don't you think? Again, and as always, the challenge of paradox.

So the poem wants to be itself; it wants to be fresh; it does not deny its DNA, but it wants to do something new also, to move on, a quality D.H. Lawrence praised in Walt Whitman: "Whitman has meant so much to me," writes Lawrence, "Whitman, the one man breaking the way ahead." And I like how Elizabeth Drew puts it, less grandly, but accurately: "The living poets carry the language forward." We have a responsibility to our time—our unprecedented time—to be of it, to contribute to it.

I like being a living poet. (Consider the alternative.) I like having work to do; I like the work and the play, the inextricable mix of the two. When my children were younger and asked me to do something I might not have anticipated, such as driving to pick them up somewhere across town on a snowy, slippery night, and I'd do it, and they'd thank me, sure, I'd say—or at least most of the time—it's my job and my joy. Poetry is my job and my joy. And I want the poem, each individual poem, to be itself. Sometimes you get the question: what's your favorite poem? The trick answer is: my next one. Maybe I will get it more right than I did last time—whatever that exactly means—and the poem will be more itself than anything I have ever written before.

The poem wants to be **complex**. Is that always true? Probably not, but when it wants to be simple, which happens, the simplicity should be a significant one. The differences between the simplicity of an experienced poet and of a beginning poet would be a study in itself.

Tom McGrath, in an interview, makes a useful distinction between a tactical and a strategic poem. The tactical poem is written for an occasion—a political demonstration, say—and it will be a poster rather than an oil painting, the very best poster you can paint, and it will serve its moment. Or that is its aim. As I say: different occasions, different responses.

I like complexity in poetry. I don't mind wrestling with the poem for its meanings; I like layers and levels. I like what Wallace Stevens says: "A poem should resist the intelligence almost successfully." I like Maurice Ravel's distinction between complexity and complication: "complexe mais pas compliqué," as he said once of a musical score.

Congestion is not complexity; it is congestion. James Wright, whom I have already quoted talking about Chinese poetry and the imaginative space he loved in it, also talks about how a recent long brilliant poem by a prominent American poet had impressed him so much, he realized that it had pressed him out flat; he didn't feel as if he had been able to live a poem: "I felt as if I'd been run over by a truck," he says. He ascribes this to "a kind of anxiety of the poet's egotism."

I see a good amount of anxious writing; the causes are often subliminal, of course, and difficult to discern, to diagnose. In contemporary poetry, some of the poets on whom the younger poets may model themselves I find wordy, too self-spectacular in their consciousness. Sometimes, I feel like echoing the Emperor in the movie *Amadeus*, who, as I remember, after hearing the young composer play a piece, declares: "Too many notes, my dear Mozart."

I want to say again: I don't mind being wrong. Philip Levine, visiting a workshop once, said that he told his students that fifty percent of what they did would go right by him because he was who he was. For myself, I am of a certain age, background, gender, experience, and the like. My tastes are very eclectic; I like many kinds of poetry, but I can't pretend there aren't things I like poetry to do, things I care less for it to do. And sometimes my reactions and decisions can be too quick.

One of my favorite stories involves (once again) Maurice Ravel, studying at the Conservatoire with Gabriel Fauré, showing his teacher the score of his string quartet—eventually one of his best-known works—and having it handed back to him rather promptly, with some disdain, by Fauré. A few days later, Fauré asked to see the score again. Ravel asked why, since his famous elder seemed to consider the work "rubbish" (that's Ravel's word). Fauré's reply? "I could have been wrong."

When poems are difficult for me, sometimes I record them, listen a few times, let them sink in and circulate in me, gradually become more intimate with them; this resembles, to some extent, the intimacy a poet experiences while bringing parts and pieces of a poem together. Such micro-work it is, such a poring over (and over and over), such a fine-tuning. When I have just occasionally written a review of a book of poetry, I have first recorded the book—a typical book will take about an hour and a half—and then listened three or four times before writing the review. With my poetry workshops, when we have, say, six or seven poems to discuss one week, in addition to other activities, such as writing together and saying poems by heart, I will usually record those poems and give their complexities (and intimacies) the best possible chance to live inside me before I write my comments on them.

One of my little tricks, when a poem seems to me to be overwritten—too many notes, too complicated, etc.—is to suggest that the poet make a version using only every other line, starting either with line one or line two—and see how fifty percent of it comes across, what is lost, what might possibly be gained. This mechanical act, the omitting of every other line, often creates incoherences, of course, with thoughts broken in half; the disjunctions can be extreme, but sometimes imaginative spaces are opened, there is room to stroll in the poem and be among its connections (a variation on James Wright's idea of imaginative space).

In Osip Mandelstams's essay on Dante, he likens the writing of a poem to crossing a river from one bank to the other by jumping onto the decks of boats that are passing in two directions. You want gaps and leaps in poetry; you also want to land on the deck of sometimes elusive boats rather than in the water between them. Exercises can, on occasion, teach us something about judging those leaps.

If I'm feeling especially devilish, I might suggest the same trick but starting with the last line, or the penultimate line, working backwards, seeing what results from that. And maybe even the left half of the poem, then the right half—see where you are typically placing your thought, see how your syntax is at work and play (or not). "Nothing to lose but your dignity," I sometimes say to my students—and perhaps to the would-be poem itself, which is having to put up with such stunts from me. Really, in the interests of shaking loose in a poem what I sense is potential within it, but is presently congealed in old habits of thought or a form that is simply not working as it might, I have no shame. If it sometimes takes this kind of prescribed / suggested frivolity behind the scenes to bring the poem to fuller life, then that's how it is going to be. Nothing to lose but your dignity.

Before I leave the theme of complexity, I want to talk about simplicity as a valid point of departure, something to bounce off, if you like, into genuine complexity. Attentiveness itself—watching, observing the so-called real world—I see as a hard surface, and I often recommend attentiveness to the younger poet as a place to proceed from. On a regular basis, be in one place, watch (with all your senses) what is going on there; be a witness of it; be faithful to what William Stafford calls "the always arriving present."

As I understand theme and variations in music—and I have favorite pieces which are "variations on a theme by," such as Brahms' variations on a theme by Handel or by Haydn, or Britten's variations on a theme by Purcell—it seems it is the basic simplicity of the theme which initiates the idea of variation in the mind of the composer. Rather than preclude complexity, the simplicity—a four-square tune, for example, even "Twinkle, Twinkle Little Star"— invites the composer's imagination to the often elaborate dance.

So, working with young writers, I'm never ashamed of simple

or basic points of departure. For me, writing assignments in the classroom have four main characteristics: everyone in the room is able to do *something* with them; they are based on poems I admire and love, or strategies I admire and love and likely use myself; they give the imagination room to move in all kinds of directions—inward, upward, outward; and, lastly, they should be *fun*. I think it was H.L. Mencken who described Puritanism as "a haunting fear that someone, somewhere may be happy." Frost says that the poet "begins in delight and ends in wisdom"; Hopkins speaks of "the fine delight that fathers thought." I know that delight and fun are not exactly synonymous, but I'd say they are in the same zone, and I believe that a good writing assignment in the classroom, at any level of experience, should strike sparks of delight (or fun or happiness) in the student writer. Not only nothing to lose but your dignity, but also, perhaps, your solemnity, also your fear of seeming ridiculous to others. When you are under way with something, grasped by it rather than grasping it (there's a big difference between the two), that kind of self-consciousness can fall away, and a new sense of freedom enters, and we begin to go somewhere, with everything to discover.

There are so many more things that the poem wants, and these are just a handful of them, as I discern it. Finally, the poem wants **more** from you—more than you might dare to think of giving as you begin. Finally, it wants **all** of you—you the writer, you the reader—the "whole soul . . . brought into being." You give it all you have, and what you have expands as you work, as you play. The imagination is a vast instrument; let us try to draw from it as much as we can, poem by poem by poem. In these attempts, writers and teachers and readers—apprentices, as we are—good luck to us all.

We began by saying a poem together; let's end the same way. Once again, I'll feed you the lines. This is one of the best pieces I know ever written by children—you can't have much more fun than this! It was written by third grade students at Wahpeton Elementary School in Wahpeton, North Dakota, during a week's visit by a poet working for the COMPAS program (Community Programs in the Arts and Sciences) of St. Paul Minnesota. Here we go:

The Luscious, Very Kissy, Smoochy Valentine Poem

Kiss me sweetheart,
I'm your brainless mudpie.
Kiss me, baby,
You're an empty piece of paper
for me to smooch
with muddy lizard fish lips.
I love you true
Like $0 + 0 = 2$ zeros,
But even math has problems!
Kiss me sweetheart,
My blue kangaroo.
I love you true
As bats hate light!
be my earthquake, darling,
Be my molten lava honeybun
And we'll spin around
Like Earth kissing Mars!
Kiss me, luscious lips,
Pulverize me,
Make me melt
Like ice cream.
Kiss me darling,
My dancing pineapple,
My rubber cement
My broccoli popsicle.
Kiss me, you fool!

"Poetry and Education" conference,
Mater Dei Institute, Dublin, Ireland,
February 2008.